WE HAVE THIS MOMENT

GLORIA GAITHER

Photography by Sue Buchanan

WORD BOOKS
PUBLISHER
WACO, TEXAS

A DIVISION OF
WORD, INCORPORATED

Library of Congress Cataloging-in-Publication Data:

Gaither, Gloria.
    We have this moment.

        1. Meditations.   2. Gaither, Gloria.   I. Title.
    BV4832.2.G242   1988   242   88-5648
    ISBN 0-8499-3120-7

Printed in the United States of America

8 9 8 AGH 9 8 7 6 5 4 3 2 1

To
WILLIAM BENJAMIN,
who has so often made me stop to
"realize life while I'm living it, every every minute."

William: The Protector; Benjamin: Favored of God

May your strength be used to protect the weak, and may
you always walk uprightly before God,
that His favor may rest on you
all the days of your life.

CAPTURING THE MOMENT

The pages of this book were never meant to be published, and the decision to do so has been an agonizing one for many reasons.

First of all, I am a hermit at heart and treasure privacy, perhaps all the more because it is such a rare commodity in my life. Also, I shrink from exposing the subtleties of my relationships to the harsh scrutiny of publicity and from revealing my weaknesses and vulnerable places.

Another reason I have hesitated to allow these pages to be read is that because they are part of a journal, written hastily on the run or under pressure, I felt they would not reflect my best writing skills. This book is not researched and rational but visceral, and the spontaneous, shorthand-like sentence structure reads more like a multimedia show than a biography or story. But that is more truly what my life is like—fragmented flashes of the many faces and hats I wear, glimpses of the places I spend my days and the seemingly unending parade of roles I play.

But I have learned that my harried lifestyle is not unique in our culture and that most of us live to a staccato beat, pulled and jerked from one role to another by the voices that invade our lives. And as in the multimedia show, it is the blending of these seemingly unrelated shots that makes up the pattern and texture of our days.

What has convinced me to become so vulnerable to you by allowing this account of my private journey to be published is the hope that you will be persuaded to begin to chronicle your own journey and by so doing discover some of what journal-keeping has taught me.

Capturing the Moment

For I have learned some surprising things from my years of journaling. First, I have discovered that what I thought at the time was of great importance in my life turned out to be not very important at all—and the regular, daily, "insignificant" events that I almost didn't bother to record have been, in hindsight, almost too poignant or beautiful to bear. Some have actually been pivotal forks in the road of my pilgrimage.

I have learned that there is eternity in every moment if I can just recognize it. Keeping a journal has sharpened my vision and is helping me, as Thornton Wilder said, "to realize life while we live it—every, every minute."

I find as I read back over these last ten years that I more often wrote about the children than the business, more about relationships than career, more about my failures than my achievements, and more about the simplicity of nature than about the possessions we accumulated.

As I look back over the pages of my journals, I see that God was at work in the regularness of my days. And because of this it has become, for me, very difficult to separate the "sacred" from the "secular" of my life. God has refused to be pigeonholed into the "religious" sector and has instead surprised me with His presence in unprescribed places and in unorthodox ways.

Because my insufficiencies far outnumber my accomplishments, I have found dependency and surrender not so much a religious exercise as it is a daily act of survival.

By the same token, what is printed here could not be considered a "prayer journal" or "spiritual diary," because most often my communication with God is so blended into the mental processes of my day that I really can't call it "prayer" in the formal sense. Instead, prayer to me has been more of an it's-you-and-me-Lord awareness that is very portable and requires no special physical pose. Often, prayer in my life has taken the forms of panicked cries for help, ecstatic exclamations of sheer joy, deep inexpressible feelings of tremendous gratitude, and the overwhelming awareness of my need.

God walks with me. And when I am least able, because of fatigue, stress, or the urgent demands on my energies by those

He brings into my life, to follow the prescribed "fundamentals of prayer" or strike a meditative pose, He scoops me up in His arms or simply sits with me in silent strength until I cannot avoid the awesome recognition that yes, even now, He is here. I have joyfully discovered that He is always "up to something" in my life, and I am learning to quit second-guessing Him and simply trust the process.

I am learning that life *is* a process. Even my very salvation is a process. True, it began years ago with a choice, but even my choosing then was embryonic. At first, I chose "in part" because "part" was all I knew. But as my choices have been confirmed by His trustworthiness, I have become a bigger risker for His sake. Indeed, I am coming to know that, paradoxically, risky living is the only safe way to go.

As you read this chronicle, you may feel that my family's lifestyle is abnormal, even perhaps exciting, because it moves from place to place. We are musicians, performers, and communicators, and we frequently go on concert tours or travel to speaking engagements or recording sessions. Interruptions are common. And because we travel so much, "home" for us has been wherever we could be together.

But what seems abnormal for some has become the norm for us. The challenge to all of us—you where you are and me where I am—is to bring consistency to the inconsistent and to create cohesion and wholeness where there is fragmentation.

In my case, I was surprised one day to discover that what the world would perceive to be our "career" almost never made my journal at all. I seldom mentioned my life on the road, concerts, or the joys and tribulations of touring. Perhaps that was because, subconsciously, I didn't consider these things "real life"—or perhaps it was the routine of it all. Discovering that I had omitted it from my account of our days made me buy another empty book just for the road and make a real effort to record my impressions when I was on tour as part of the Bill Gaither Trio.

But my journal revealed that, in spite of what the public might think, the "real stuff" took place at home, and even when I was away, I was always trying to "make home" in foreign places.

I learned that what sociologists call "primary relationships" really are primary, and that my Lord and my family are a treasure more priceless than gold.

I learned that it is true that one of the most urgent and fundamental needs of human beings is the need to belong, to really matter, and to have an identity uniquely one's own but in the context of a caring community—to know where one comes from and to truly believe one has someplace to go.

I have come to believe that one of the crying needs in me, and in our culture in general, is the need for silence and solitude. But the pressures and pace of our society teach us to shrink from silence and contemplation. Reflection and introspection are not highly valued, and they even frighten us a little.

It scares me to realize that so many in our country reach young adulthood having never made friends with silence and are uncomfortable when they find themselves alone. Sound pollution has conditioned us to ignore the cacophony, yet our bodies react to the onslaught with their defense mechanisms, releasing hormones and enzymes that were meant to protect us only in times of occasional high stress or crisis. And since we were not intended to be subjected to such a sustained bombardment, our organs and nervous systems often suffer from the overload.

How we need the healing balm of silence! Now, more than ever, our spirits whisper to us to stop and be still by bringing to our consciousness the awareness that something is missing, that there is a void that must be filled. Even though our culture has conditioned us to equate success with being busy and scheduled, deep down we know that running faster, staying occupied, moving and climbing, and filling all the spaces with the giddy sounds of our own voices will never really soothe the gnawing awareness that something is wrong at the core of our being.

My journal has revealed in me this insatiable thirst for silence—and a deep gratitude for the gift of it. I have learned that "meditation" and "centering" are not words to fear, but needs as innate and as ancient as Adam and Eve, who knew the first day after creation was completed that communing in the still of the evening was a necessary part of life.

Capturing the Moment

Silence by itself is restorative. But even better is silence coupled with reflection, a time to contemplate the moment, to assess one's position and progress, to internalize the details and the subtleties of the situation. Nothing is better for contemplation than writing down, however simply, the events we experience and the way we feel about them. We remember more of what we record and it becomes a part of us, much as children remember what took place when they were very small if those events were recorded in photographs placed in a well-used scrapbook.

The traveler with the camera around his neck has become a comic stereotype of tourists around the world. How wonderful it would be if little empty books could become as common and as necessary to the sojourner as unexposed film and fail-safe cameras!

And yet I hope we don't throw away our cameras—photographs can be wonderful tools for capturing moments, too! My friend Sue Buchanan has been using her camera this way for many years. And so I have asked her to add another dimension to this book by sharing some of her photos and suggesting some ways to use photography as a journaling device. Her ideas are found in the section entitled "Photographic Memories."

The truth is, we need both journals and cameras to make us stop and focus—so our moments don't pass us by. Elizabeth O'Connor, in her book, *Cry Pain, Cry Hope,* says of contemplation and reflection:

> It is not what happens to us in any day that gives content to our lives, but whether or not we let its experience sink into us. As Moses learned, reflection is essential to that process. It is one of the highest powers given to anyone. In reflection, I came upon feelings that I had been too afraid to experience in the moment. In the quiet of reflection I take the risk and the time to let censored thoughts as well as feelings into consciousness, to discover what is causing the uneasiness in me.*

*Elizabeth O'Connor, *Cry Pain, Cry Hope* (Waco, TX: Word Books, 1987), p. 33.

Last, I would like to give a word of advice about the logistics of keeping a journal. First, I have found it best to use an empty book instead of a commercial diary, because diaries are too restricting. They make us feel guilty if we don't write in them every day, and then, when we do write, they limit the space so that we aren't free to write out the content of our hearts. I prefer empty books that are small enough to be portable but large enough to give a feeling of space.

Don't let journal keeping become a tyrant to you! Your journal is your friend. It will hear your thoughts when no one else will. You can always be honest, and a journal holds over you no criteria for proper or creative writing. Write short. Write long. Write often. Write not at all. The journal is there, patient as an old dog, always friendly and receptive when you're ready to talk. And when you want to listen, it will tell you things about yourself you never dreamed. You may discover flaws you didn't know you had. But more likely, you will discover to your great joy a depth in yourself you didn't know was there.

The journals from which this book is excerpted span ten years of incredible changes in my life. Our children were seven, eight, and twelve when this decade began and were seventeen, eighteen, and twenty-two when it ended. They went from elementary school to college and graduate work, and to me they grew from being children to being friends. During these years I experienced an amazing metamorphosis as a woman and as a person. Bill and I weathered many a storm and grew in ways I am now forced to declare nothing less than miraculous.

In short, these were what is referred to as the high-production years, the frantic, demanding summertime of life. Out of these years came a song that most accurately characterizes what I learned and would say to you if I could pass on one message:

> . . . We have this moment to hold in our hands
> And to touch as it slips through our fingers like sand;
> Yesterday's gone, and tomorrow may never come,
> But we have this moment—today!

PHOTOGRAPHIC MEMORIES

The pictures in this book were never meant to be published, and the decision to do so has been an agonizing one . . . sound familiar?

My first reaction when Gloria asked me to participate in this book was "I'm not a photographer" . . . but that's not true, since that's exactly what I am by profession. Actually, I call myself a "producer-director." My company is a visual production company (film, multi-image, and video), and my job is "getting" the picture and making it part of a production. While I'm not always the one to click the shutter or roll the film, I'm forever looking through the viewfinder and making the judgment call. That's my "best stuff" . . . not what you see in this book, which are snapshots taken just as Gloria wrote—"hastily on the run or under pressure" and sometimes out of focus.

For the past six months, various-sized envelopes have arrived from Gloria—sections of this book for me to match with photos. I've frantically tried to pair up my photos to her entries—and it just didn't work.

But today a final skinny envelope arrived . . . the introduction to all that came before. And for the first time I discovered that although the two of us have feelings that are parallel at certain moments in our lives, my photographic journey will never perfectly match Gloria's written journal—and neither do I have to "visualize" a "script."

Photographic Memories

Life is interpretation. An artist uses a brush; a poet, verse; a musician, his or her instrument. And most creative works turn out to be private . . . or at most seen or heard by one's family or closest friends.

Gloria never dreamed as she wrote in her journals that these emotions would be so exposed, just as I never expected to explain my picture that was chosen to parallel her journal entry.

I had taken my grownup daughter with me to New York City to write the script for a show I was producing there. This was the first time we'd worked together professionally. We were having breakfast in the little cafe "Un Deux Trois," where each table comes equipped with a paper tablecloth and a box of crayons. As two very adult women discussed the project that brought us there, the child in her pushed aside her coffee cup and began to draw . . . and the "chronicler" in me grabbed my camera (close at hand for professional reasons) to record the event.

In reading Gloria's introduction, I realize that we share the same insecurities in "laying out there" for the world to see something that is very private. And much in line with Gloria's thoughts about encouraging you to begin a journal, I had made notes along the way to encourage you to "keep a record" photographically of signposts in life . . . of logs and garden swings and discarded toy soldiers along with the usual happy birthdays and merry Christmases.

With that in mind, let me continue with my first lesson. First, photography is 95 percent in the eye of the photographer; the other 5 percent can be learned easily by trial and error and from your local camera shop clerk. So . . . get a camera—even a cheap one will do. With your very first roll of film, snap a half-roll of pictures (various angles, of course) of the garden swing you played on with your sister when you were children. Use the other half of the roll to shoot Aunt Alice's prize rose (you'll always remember Aunt Alice for her roses).

Now have the film developed; choose the best two compositions, and have two enlargements made of each. You are well on your way.

Photographic Memories

The two extra prints? Oh yes! They are for your sister and Aunt Alice. Why not frame them for their birthdays? Even lousy photography will look great matted in black with a simple gold frame.

This summer I went with my husband to his high school reunion. While he reminisced with his friends, I headed off with my camera to shoot the local "landmarks" in his hometown. When Christmas or his birthday comes around and I can't think of a thing to give him, I'll present him with a half-dozen framed photographs of one of his "favorite places in the world" . . . Dana, Indiana (including my favorite . . . a "kiss the hog" contest sign in the post office window!).

Whatever the means you use—writing, photography, or something else—record the moment in a journal of your own. That's what Gloria and I did—ours just happens to be "published."

SUE BUCHANAN

Hold tight to the sound of the music of living,
Happy songs from the laughter of children at play;
Hold my hand as we run through the sweet fragrant meadows,
Making mem'ries of what was today.

Tiny voice that I hear is my little girl calling
For daddy to hear just what she has to say;
And my little son running there by the hillside
May never be quite like today.

Tender words, gentle touch, and a good cup of coffee,
And someone that loves me and wants me to stay;
Hold them near while they're here, and don't wait for tomorrow
To look back and wish for today.

Take the blue of the sky and the green of the forest
And the gold and the brown of the freshly mown hay,
Add the pale shades of spring and the circus of autumn,
And weave you a lovely today.

For we have this moment to hold in our hands
And to touch as it slips through our fingers like sand;
Yesterday's gone, and tomorrow may never come,
But we have this moment —today!

1977

There is something within me that whispers
when I see the ocean,
"This is where your heart is at home.". . .

July 26 — Nantucket

Today I have selfishly stolen away to the pond near the jetties to watch the creatures who live here and to be *their* guest. I hope they don't mind. I hope after I leave there will be hours of solitude for them.

The water lilies are lovely in the morning sun—some pink and some white, deepening to ivory, then yellow at the center. Occasionally, sea gulls soar by overhead, while unconcerned turtles sun themselves on abandoned wood planks floating among the lily pads.

I wanted Amy to come here with me—I thought she might enjoy this place. But she was pouting a bit because I had told her not to holler in the courtyard. It hurt me when I asked her if she'd like to come and she said, "No," not lifting her eyes to mine.

A year ago she would not have asserted herself to turn down anyone's request for fear of hurting that person. And so she was always being hurt by others, who didn't always reciprocate. I guess I should have felt good that she is daring to say what she feels, but I didn't. I felt that some of her idealism at life had slipped away—some of her trust, some of her belief in goodness.

And I felt rejection, too, that she was choosing a chance to be with her friends over a cozy time with me—something she used to drop everything for. It wasn't that I wanted her to go if she didn't want to. It was just that I wanted her to want to.

I'm not good at being a mother. I don't like doing what's best sometimes instead of what I feel. I don't like disciplining and correcting when I feel like ignoring and hugging. I don't like it that sweet, polite, thoughtful children and disciplined, considerate adults come only as a result of *some* unpleasant moments.

But I dislike the alternative even more. I dislike loud, rude, inconsiderate children and sloppy, rude, and careless adults who don't respect themselves or anyone else. So I guess I'll go on correcting and disciplining and sometimes being rejected because of it.

July 30 — Nantucket

All good things come to an end, sometimes giving way to things even better.

I feel my mind bracing itself for re-entry into the real world. My spirit, though, has been refreshed, and I am more fitted to the task than I was when I came here. One cannot be so close to the sea without being restored.

There is something within me that whispers when I see the ocean, "This is where your heart is at home." I think my soul is made of salt water that flows to itself when released from the casement of circumstances. Surely, the sea flows to eternity—and when we get to heaven we will truly be "on the other shore," but by the sea nonetheless.

This week the sea has reminded me to trust the ebb and flow of the tides. It is easy in relationships to think that the high tide is the norm. I must remember that the tide which recedes will surely return. I can trust the process and not feel deserted when the waters leave nor threatened when they return. "The tide rises and the tide falls."

August 9 — home

We came straight home from Nantucket to a week of rehearsals and hard work, but we all feel excited about the possibilities of the fall.

Amy saw a hummingbird yesterday—in our own backyard! It was early, and we were sitting in the garden swing reading a

book when she noticed it—tiny, greenish, flitting incredibly forward and backward around and through the scotch pine. We'd never seen one here before.

After all the work to plant the trees—watering, nurturing, waiting—the birds are returning! And the smell. . . like the Michigan north woods of my childhood.

Bill insisted on these pine trees. Bless him!

1978

In our heads we know, but with our days we deny,
that great deeds are only and always the result of great ideas,
and that ideas demand time, effort, and devotion . . . .

January 10 — home

Has it really been this long since I've written in this book? Yet when I look back over it, the months seem like years because so much has happened.

The growth that has been a part of our lives—almost forced upon us like birth—has been both pain and glory. But, my, how we've aged! It's strange about aging spiritually, though. Instead of *losing* innocence and trust, as one does from mere physical maturing, one gains them. The more miles you have on you from the travels of the heart, the more simple and childlike your faith becomes. I *believe* today as never before.

January 26 — home

There was a terrible blizzard all night with thirty- to forty-mile-per-hour winds. Everything is closed today—schools, businesses, even the Delco-Remy plant. The drifts are up to a man's waist and higher, the temperature is zero degrees, and the wind-chill factor threatens at minus fifty. The poor little birds keep crashing into the windows trying to find a place to hide from the storm. We haven't had any twenty below days, but the snow and wind have been worse. I'm so thankful I thought to stock up on milk, juice, and groceries.

The kids don't mind at all. They're just glad to be home, warm, and by the fire. Later we will try to get out to give water to the dogs and unplug the back door. We can't even get the door open for the drifts.

January 29 — home

Little did we know what "getting out" would mean. There are drifts ten to fifteen feet tall all around the car. The snow is waist-deep in most other places. Even Aunt Lillie* says she's never seen anything like it.

Suzanne and I managed to make it to Mother's to feed the ducks. It was almost impossible to get to the duck house and so exhausting to try. The air is so cold (six degrees with wind chill of minus twenty-six degrees) that we had to have our faces covered in order to breathe, and we sank in to the hip with each step.

People have frozen to death; most were those who left their cars or powerless houses to go for help. But mostly the cold's just been paralyzing. Whole cities are shut down. The mayor of Indianapolis has been on TV begging people to stay off the streets. Hundreds of deserted cars are having to be towed out of the roads and interstates before plowing can even begin. Many private citizens with plows, four-wheel-drive vehicles, and snowmobiles have been helping with emergency deliveries.

We've been very thankful to be at home with plenty of food, plenty of wood and fuel, and each other. Benjy's been drawing dinosaurs. He knows them all by name and habit. Suzanne's kept in contact with her friends and helped shovel out and feed the animals. Amy has been helping in the kitchen, making cookies, clearing the table, and dancing about. Bill keeps three fires going (even all night) and fills the wood boxes.

February 1 — home

We had a wonderful week together. Did all the things we never have time to do: finger paint, cornstarch clay, soap carving,

*Bill's great aunt, sister to his Dad's mother.

valentines, cookies, table games, and macaroni letter signs.

We had good breakfasts and plenty of time to eat together. (Amy at supper: "I wish I could speed-read. Stacy went to Chicago for a whole week and speed-read." Benjy: "Who won?")

We drug out all the old Smothers Brothers records and had sore bellies from laughing.

The children are back in school today—but *mountains* of snow line the narrow lanes the plows have dug out. And it's still only seven degrees. If the groundhog has any brains, he won't even come out tomorrow, let alone look for his shadow!

It's snowing again. Bill said that after last week there will either be a lot of divorces next week or a lot of babies next October.

March 9 — home

Suzanne is fourteen and seems to have become a young woman overnight. It's been exciting, yet scary, watching her. Bill has had a bit of a trauma recognizing it.

She has a little boyfriend—a nice kid who wants to serve the Lord, I think. She seems too young to me, yet she needs to learn gradually how to be in control of situations and of herself. She can only learn by having a chance to try.

I'm leading a six-week series for youth at the church—partly because I want to know that youth group myself before I let Suzanne get very involved. I want to make some personal evaluations of the leaders and see what the values of the group are.

I do love kids! I really enjoy them and empathize with their hurts and joys. In fact, I wonder if one ever gets through with adolescence. Half the time I myself still teeter between wanting to quit and run and being excited about plunging headlong into some new uncharted territory. I'm grateful that my curiosity and circumstances usually shove me on. I think that is good, so long as I have first chosen my direction and carefully charted the course so that I am not forced into oblivion by not having a "flight plan."

April 17 — home

What a beautiful morning! I'm up early to speak to an elementary school in Anderson. The sun is drying off the little bit of frost we had last night, the birds are singing, and spring is really here at last.

The daffodils have been outrageous this year—so many, and so welcome. The waterfowl are sitting on their nests now, and the swamp willows are beginning to leaf out to hide them.

It is springtime in our spirits, too, and after a long winter—both physical and spiritual—we are experiencing a real strength and victory in knowing we have obeyed God and our commitment is true.

Yesterday, Bill and I stayed home to work on some songs and finished one called "I Am Loved." Wrote another this week we will call "I Will Go On."

May 6 — on tour, in the air between Omaha and Denver

One night of our long tour is behind us. It was a good night, and the people were the most responsive they've ever been in Omaha.

Bill and I called home after the concert. It was especially good to talk to Suzanne, who has been through the first rocky stages of maturing these last few months. Yes, she has grown, and how I love her, ache for her, dream for her.

I, too, am growing and seem to be at a plateau as a person. At times I'm happy with myself and what I know about myself. At other times, I'm frustrated with my failures and lack of confidence.

Sometimes I feel that Bill doesn't take me seriously. But I am just beginning to recognize that many times this is not so much because I am not enough for him, but because I'm too much for him.

Always before, when these little conflicts have occurred, I have gone away convinced I was not mature or intelligent or rational or objective enough. But lately I felt myself turn a corner of discovery. I am mature and objective and intelligent. Sometimes that is too much of a force to be reckoned with, and it is easier to dismiss me than have me there to muddy the waters with my questions and probes.

I don't blame him. I do the same thing when I have some nice little system all worked out and I don't want to be bothered with someone poking holes in it or casting doubt on my reason.

I am learning to be willing to subject myself to pain in order to buy discovery. I want to walk on the precarious sea of self-investigation in order to reach the shore of contentment with what I have accomplished.

I really love Bill and have a deep appreciation for the load he carries. I respect his discipline and willingness to risk.

Somehow I must support and respect his strength without letting my own strengths be swallowed and negated by them. If I allow that to happen, I will lose not only my self-respect, but his respect as well.

We are both gentle "heavies" and will always have to work at preserving one another as well as challenging each other.

May 10 — on tour, Los Angeles

The children are coming here tonight. I'm so anxious to hold them in my arms again and see their faces. Seems as if we've been gone forever, yet the quiet and rest we've had the last few days has been good. We all had colds, flu, and sore throats, all of which disappeared after a day of rest and sun and fruit. Bill and I so needed this time, too. Pressures and the necessities of life both get our attention. It's good to be able to focus in on each other again.

Benjy is so excited about hitting a ball to the fence in T-league. Suzanne and Amy are thankful to have their work done ahead of time for the trip. We have a good life—an exciting yet astoundingly simple life. May we never get to the place where we cannot rejoice in simplicity!

May 17 — still on tour, Nampa, Idaho

Only four more days to go! The troops are tired, but the concert last night was especially warm, and the people responded.

I missed the kids yesterday. Seems harder after having had them with us. Called home this morning. Suzanne got an "A" on her science test and all "A's" so far in English. Amy and Benjy are both all caught up with their work and eager to get going in Little League.

A wild summer is about to begin . . .

June 26 — home

At the church convention there is a bookstore tent filled with
cards, records, books, and materials. But the counter that draws
the children back each year with their summer savings is the
Christian trinket department.

Over and over again I've warned the children not to spend their
money foolishly—and time and time again they've come home
with plastic key rings, polyethylene squeeze-together coin purses,
combs and mirrors, finger-spinning tops, and worthless yo-yos.

The thing that inevitably lures these normally sensible
youngsters into their purchases is the fact that somewhere on
each item is etched a gold-lettered Bible text or glow-in-the-dark
praying hands. This fact also pricks my conscience months later
and prevents me from raking up the lot of them and filling up
the trash-smasher.

This year I determined to avoid the problem—at least with
Suzanne, since she is now a teenager. We had a talk about using
her money on something of real value, even if she had to spend
more for it. She promised she would purchase with care.

When she came home from the convention grounds that day,
she couldn't wait to show me.

"I spent my whole amount, Mother," she said, "but it was worth
it. I think it's real pewter. It even came in a velvet box." She held

up her "Witness Cross" for me to see, then snapped it around her neck.

I congratulated her for choosing something nice, then tapped the new treasure with a coin to hear the ring of metal on metal to affirm her wisdom. But the flat sound was not the clear ring we expected.

Plastic. Molded plastic. Foiled again! Shaped like a cross, colored like pewter—but it was only a fake replica. I guess one can't always tell.

I hope I remember to transfer this little insight into life. Just having the shape or sound or appearance of being religious does not make something real. We must examine everything in the revealing light of God's word.

Jesus bids us "touch and see." We must not trade the golden essence of faith for pretense, form, sham, and replicas. We must taste and see, touch and feel, test the spirits. We must not settle for less than the real substance of life God has for us.

July 8 — home

In the pines some lovely bird is singing about the rain last night.

We're all thankful for it: the garden, the birds, the trees, the farmers, and me. I would like to sing about it, too, but someone would be sure to look at me funny—a middle-aged housewife pirouetting about the yard, expressing my joy in some slightly under-the-tone tune.

Birds don't worry about things like that. No one ever says, "Sparrows should keep still and let the cardinals have it." Or, "Isn't that silly for that robin to think he can sing! Really! Someone close to him should clue him in that he should stick to sticks and straws."

I think of the macaws. A friend of ours who just returned from Peru says the jungle is alive with marvelous sounds. "Music," he called it. "All day symphonies," he said.

And yet if parrots and macaws and cockatoos were sensible

creatures, they'd be silenced and reminded of their "shortcomings" by "someone close." Gracious! Have you ever heard one solo?

But I think it's not for exhibiting vocal perfection that birds sing. I think they have to sing to live! Literally. All the passions and necessities of their lives are attached to their sounds.

Inhibition is an ailment peculiar to human beings alone, a contagion caught from a carrier who most often does not suffer from the symptoms himself, but infects others with the disease . . . most often at a time in life when resistance is lowest.

We who must sing to live must keep our spiritual resistance high. Feast on the positive nourishment of God's word. Delight in the good things of the Lord, then let the music flow!

August 1 — home

Amy and I had a long talk about the facts of life this week. I tried to lift the curtain of miracle for her and let her know that entering puberty is like crossing the threshold from the outer courtyard of innocence into the very holy of holies itself, experiencing with that step the pain and glory that comes with knowledge and responsibility. To realize that she carries in her body the potential to be co-creator with the God of the universe is an awesome and yet wonderful realization.

The laughter and tears that burst simultaneously from her little upturned face told me what an earthshaking moment this was for her. For me, this was one of the unique moments of my life that makes me thrilled, thankful, and scared to death to be a mother.

Together we prayed that she would keep her vessel pure and clean. And we prayed for the child somewhere entering manhood who will someday be her husband—that God would protect and preserve him and bring him one day to her, so that together they could buck the tide of careless living to form a home that will be fortress and citadel, cathedral and synagogue, laughter and healing to some other child.

August 21 — Beaver Island on Lake Michigan

Curtain call to summer. Seems as though the action should be only beginning. School starts this week, but the children will miss a couple of days for this more important education: pines against the blue, blue sky; white sails slithering between resting white gulls; quaint little buildings in a cluster along the northeast cove, huddled together as a protection against the tides—both of the surf and of the world.

The buildings here are simple, practical structures, preserved and cared for but without trim and frills, painted to protect against wind and weather—mostly white because white paint is cheaper and less complicated to bring from the mainland.

This is not a place of abundant options. Necessities are available and a few pleasures, but bared, pared down to basics. No hype. No extras.

Ferry ride: simple, awkward tub of a boat, blunt and high like Noah's ark, with us as animals hanging from our little corners of the deck. Water stormy—tossing us like marbles in a cup—and not even a raven to send ashore.

A car ride through the virgin timber; hot dogs beside a hidden lake; sunset on the beach . . . alone.

Benjy and Amy racing down the dunes to scoot on their bottoms to the water's edge. Unstoppable squeals!

Suzanne alone . . . piling sand, thinking, changing, turning, yet still hanging on to childhood.

Bicycle rides to the village. An outrageous liquid crimson moon, rising out of a satin sea fresh from the moon-vat, still dripping until suspended and attached to the black, number-four sandpaper sky.

Deserted beach, the greedy gulls' feeding ground, littered with man's refuse: T-bones, sardines, chicken bones, bread crusts, and my apple coffeecake. I pay toll for crossing to their side of the island—little cold stream, cold enough to numb bare feet.

The children and I skip rocks. Perfect rocks, worn to paper thinness, that skip two, three, four times, with practice. A small excited voice: "Everybody throw when I say, 'Three!' One. Two. Three!"

Old abandoned car. Still has wooden spoked wheels and running boards. Good wood outlasts good metal.

Monarchs and bank swallows flit between my thoughts. Smell of cedar pushes back my efforts.

Sausage and sunrise form an easy alliance, forged together with the aroma of hot coffee and comfortable relationships; cottages warmed by itinerant children, moving from love to love.

The calls of loons, gulls, nightingales, human voices drowned out by the insistent silence and the drama of the setting sun.

Line by line, moment by moment, this week is etched into our memories in the permanent ink of the everlasting love in these relationships! This week, a masterpiece in scrimshaw, to be treasured and preserved.

December 30 — Key Biscayne

It has been months since I've picked up this journal. Why do I only seem to find time for reflection when I'm on vacation, away from the mainstream of my life?

There is nothing wrong with contemplation. So why does it take at least three days to take away the guilt of doing it? What is it that makes us Americans feel that time is wasted that is not filled with pointless motion, aimless busyness?

In our heads we know, but with our days we deny, that great deeds are only and always the result of great ideas, and that ideas demand time, effort, and devotion just as surely as the doing of the deeds.

Today I will dream and not feel accused by some faceless tyrant. I will pioneer in the trackless, unexplored territory of my soul and will not be afraid.

December 31 — Key Biscayne

The sun doesn't shine everywhere the same.

I never paid much attention when my view was obstructed by buildings and traffic lights. But here, at the ocean, I can see forever, and though the clouds are thick above me and the land where I sit is gray, I can see that the ocean has stripes of sunlight far away. What interesting texture they give to the speckled fabric of the water's surface!

Not that I don't find beauty in sparkling glass. But for today striped tweed will suit me fine.

1979

Listen to the stillness, more audible than any sound....

April 20 — Pittsburgh, Pennsylvania

This has been a rocky season for my emotions. Aspiration and frustration running rampant in the cage of what I have become. Blessing and curse—Siamese twins, so vitally joined they are inoperable. Bittersweet success holds brambles on its branches, and the thorns entwine themselves across the picket gate from which the best and yet-to-fly in me longs to escape.

I have learned how to be honest. Yet the price of honesty is often that the scalpel of my words injures the ones I hold most dear—the ones who hurt me most. So pain is not an option. Either way it shares my days.

Yet it's been a beautiful day. Spring will bring new life, and caged birds do fly.

June 27 — home

A moment of quiet. The doves are melancholy, yet the breeze seems content. My heart can understand them both and, like nature, lets both dwell together without conflict.

Amy has recovered from another minor surgery. We've taken an exhausting trip to Holland. The church convention is passed, and a new album is staring me in the face on Monday morning. It takes all I have and all the grace God can give me to hear "peace" whispered to my soul and stomach. But one day I will look back and see that I have grown and conquered more rough terrain.

The cabin is nearing completion. I am eager to spend time and manual labor making a nest so that my mind will have a place to lay its eggs and hatch its brood. I know there are some fertile seeds in me if I can just give them a place to incubate.

July 29 — home

Just came back from the cabin. What a place for restoration! I've been working out there off and on and about have everything tucked into place.

This morning Suzanne and I went out early to pick berries, but it began to rain. I put on coffee, and we played Pick-Up Sticks and Scrabble until Bill came out with his folks. Then we spent the morning on the porch watching the rain, sipping coffee, and being close to nature. How I love that place! So close to home, yet so isolated and peaceful.

We really miss Amy, who is in Michigan fishing with Mother. Seems as if she's been gone forever. We've decided not to spend the night at the cabin until she gets home.

We have to go back one more time to work on the album. It will be good if we ever get it done. This one has been very difficult, but we keep at it. The schedule has really worked out

quite well, because the children have recorded, too, working on
a different project, so at least we've been together.

Suzanne marched with the band in a parade today—in the rain.
Today was also the end of the 4-H Fair.

How I love the simple things!

August 7 — home

Bill and I are alone this week. Suzanne is at band camp; Amy and
Benjy are in Nashville recording. We went out last night and rode
all over central Indiana through the back roads.

We loved being together, and when we came home we made
love on the deck under the moon. It was so humid there was a
fog, and the pines and magnolia have reached high enough to
surround the deck with shelter and a breeze.

I gave some thought to what it will be like when the two of us
are alone again and the children are involved with lives of their
own. I hope we keep close through the years, so we won't have
to use the children to camouflage estrangement. I hope we are
still so in love that the children will feel a freedom from and a
magnetism to home—feeling welcome when they are here yet
not guilty when they are away.

Now is the time to begin my own preschool lessons in letting
go. And it is a joy to watch what our kids are becoming. Still,
we'll be glad to have them home and snug.

Meanwhile, I savor the silence and listen to the truth that
nature whispers, yielding myself, as Emerson says, "to the
perfect whole." The trees are full of little birds that are, I think,
tufted titmice (is that the plural?). They are gray with a white
breast and a black-striped head and are crested. They could also
be white-breasted nuthatches. They sound like a roomful of little
calculators, setting up a rhythm base for a unique symphony. A
fiery cardinal sings a solo above the brook and the locusts, and
occasionally, just for emphasis, a distant jay injects his funky
lick—as if the sounds were being mixed by some divine engineer
in this exclusive forest studio.

August 29 — the cabin

Listen to the stillness, more audible than any sound—not tinny like so many sounds I hear these days. The silence is full and rich, demanding that I listen and suggesting always that I'd be a fool not to. Only fools refuse the counsel of the wise, and this silence seems to know everything.

Maybe it's the oaks and beeches. They've seen the fleet-footed native Indian children tossing pebbles at their roots and chasing little fawns around between them. They've stood and heard the council casting lots for war or peace while fragrant pipe smoke wafted through their branches. These oaks have housed a thousand generations of owls and jays, withstood abuse from woodpeckers and men.

Perhaps it is the brook, whispering of its secret travels, nurturing the earth along its way.

And maybe it's the earth—the pregnant, fertile earth—pulling me like influential kin back to my moorings and my heritage.

And I *have* been a prodigal, traipsing along behind the band just like a thoughtless gypsy anywhere the living was easy . . . stealing morsels when I could have had the loaf. But there is a catch to that kind of life—and until now I've chosen not to pay the price of coming home to the plenty of the simple.

Simplicity is single—one voice asking such a pointed question. And here in silence, the only sound to hear is my own answer. Will I come back and inherit the earth?

September 27 — the cabin

The year has slipped across the crest and is rolling headlong down the winter side. Today I had to build fires in the stove and fireplace and nurse them home to comfort. The damp woods are wonderful with the scent of cedar smoke in the air. I'll fix some supper here and bring the children out after school.

The spiders have built bridges between every picket on the porch fence and between each slat on the log chairs. The spiders march along like little soldiers on patrol, always alert and ready to make attack on any intruders. But their practical life-and-death defenses look magical to me, like strands of golden silk hung in an affluent turn-of-the-century parlor.

December 28 — home

It was a lovely Christmas. We stayed home and did a lot of fun things with family and friends, like seeing the musical, *Annie!* again for the third time, going to a Globetrotters game, and having people at the house.

Some people say Christmas is a farce, a commercial gimmick to force us by social pressure to spend money for people we don't like on things they can't use.

I rebel at that. I'm thankful for a chance to say "love" in special ways to people who would think such gifts strange if Christmas didn't give us an excuse. I love the work and fuss, the planning and decorating.

Christmas is a time of decency and tenderness. I pray that greed, selfishness, and cynicism will never tarnish its golden glory or eclipse its simple message.

1980

Blessed! I am so blessed — and so responsible!

January 24 — home

In high school when I was reading Huxley's *Brave New World* and *1984*, George Orwell's terrifying novel of the future, I was certain they were fantasy, because I thought this world would never stand to see such decadence and confused values.

Now I stand on the threshold of the decade Orwell was writing about. And *Brave New World* doesn't seem like fantasy anymore; its values have become almost commonplace.

Family unity and lifelong monogamy have turned out to be the things that approach fantasy. The word *mother* has indeed become a shortened version of the basest obscenity, and children are permitted (by law in some states) to engage in sexual experimentation, including sexual intercourse, for the sake of (would you believe it?) mental health, personal freedom, and emotional security.

Uterine exterminations of babies are allowed on the basis of the whim to eliminate children of nonpreferable sex. And there is serious talk of "cleansing" our cluttered world of the physically and mentally deficient at birth as well as "allowing" those whose life span has outrun their commercial usefulness the "right" to die.

The emerging generation is unaware of its "coming out" because much of it has chosen to drug itself into oblivion to avoid the pain of the world in which it must live. And the genetic outcome of the drug culture is yet to be predicted or realized.

The industrialized nations' scramble for energy is building a scorching fire under the volatile and potentially explosive Middle East, while the nuclear stockpiles of the world threaten to annihilate all life in an Armageddon that would indeed cause the "sky to roll back like a scroll" (or more like a singed toenail) as the protective ozone layer is fried away.

Yet despite all this, overwhelming victory is ours through Christ Jesus our Lord!

Amy, Benjy, and Suzanne are growing, maturing, developing in exciting ways every day, even though they live in the midst of a "perverse generation."

People are listening to the Good News more eagerly than ever before. And as a result of the tremendous demand the world makes on Christians to exercise and keep spiritually fit, the body of Christ is developing a muscle of faith like I have never before seen.

The resulting courage and stamina have taken the people of God marching fearlessly into every fiery furnace and lion's den of the modern world. Many a Red Sea has been parted and many a desert has been conquered because of the nourishment gained from the manna gathered in clandestine meetings around the globe. And often these were meetings of God's Army of the Committed across traditional battle lines.

God has always had a people. He does now. Life is *still* worth living, because it is not affected by external circumstances. On to the conquering of inner and outer space!

May 21 — in the air

We're flying to England to begin our tour of the United Kingdom and the Netherlands. This flight has taken all day and all night, and we will arrive at 9:40 A.M. London time. Even with little or no sleep, the children and the band are in good spirits and very excited as we prepare to land. Our first concert will be tonight with no rest, but right now we feel restored by short naps and anticipation. Our land transportation will be by tour bus.

Later that day — London

Tiny houses, small walled-in gardens of larkspur and roses. Narrow streets lined with some species of sycamore and chestnut. The chestnuts bloom fire pink.

Our hotel has small rooms with single beds and is right across from Hyde Park.

May 22 — London

Last night's concert was very surprising. The people were ecstatic and very responsive afterward. We couldn't believe it! The interviewers said they had never seen an English audience respond like that.

Amy, Benjy, and I had breakfast at a tiny Italian restaurant—pastry and coffee and milk. The coffee was the greatest, like cappuccino with milk. The walk through the London streets was like walking into a novel: double-decker buses and small, unfamiliar cars; "bobbies" and chamber maids; little sidewalk cafes and window boxes full of phlox and geraniums; chestnuts in bloom; and children in the park. Women of the night scurried past the proper ladies doing their morning shopping, never giving each other a glance of recognition of what they share in common.

I went into a little bookshop for a copy of *A Writer's Britain*. So

eager to find and visit Thomas Hardy country. The bus is a
fine way to go!

Same day — on the bus

The gentle English countryside—rolling shades of green outlined
in smoky privet; and vast, brilliant patches of sunny mustard.
Thatch-roofed farm houses and gorgeous barns of practical brick.

Everything so neat and careful. Careful buildings, careful
hedges, careful compact streets and farms.

Proper, satisfied-with-itself England. And most self-satisfied of
all are the narrow Gothic churches outweighing the small villages
with their solemnity and size, aloof and compatible with the dead
who keep them company.

May 23 — to Manchester via Stratford

We stopped at Stratford on Avon, William Shakespeare's home. Bill
was quiet. His foot, which he had injured at home, was sore, and
he was upset with me for wanting to leave earlier to come here.

Perhaps I should not have urged Bill. I mustn't impose my
dreams and longings on him. I must learn to live the moment
and be grateful for what it brings, asking no more. I must learn
to be a taster, to sip and be satisfied with just a hint of flavor
on my tongue.

That's hard for me. It is my nature to drain right to the dregs
the cup of every day and feel the heady intoxication of drinking
deep the joy!

This little village is ancient and compact, like a scale miniature
in which one can actually shrink—like Alice with her
mushroom—and walk about. We walk along a cobbled path into
the church graveyard where ancient bones are laid and enter the
stoic, stone-walled church with its crannied nooks for holy men

to sit in narrow pose. We cast our ten pence in the box as toll to enter the sanctum of Shakespeare and his family. Our donation (the posted blue sheet explains) is to keep the dust of the living from gathering on the dust of the dead.

Same day — Manchester

We drive through little villages, their plain and practical women doing the morning marketing with bandanas tied beneath their chins. Travelers in their tiny cars stop beside the road to stretch their legs and munch on mutton sandwiches, while rosy-cheeked children romp there in the roadside grass.

May 25 — on the ferry to Belfast

We traveled across breathtaking country to the coast of Scotland and up along the rugged Atlantic, then took the ferry from the northern bay to Northern Ireland.

Many British soldiers are on this boat. Officers eat in the dining room, a lovely room where we had a leisurely lunch. Smooth passage. We arrive in Ireland and drive through the countryside to Belfast. The trouble here seems to have calmed down some. The soldiers are maintaining a very low profile, and the local police are trying to keep the peace.

May 26 — Belfast

As we ride through the city, we see several bombed-out buildings and barbed-wire rooftops. Today is a bank holiday here, so there is little traffic or activity on the streets. Most shops are closed.

We did an interview on the BBC. Tight security, but the airways seem very free. People, regular Irish people, seem to be trying very hard to live as if it were "business as usual."

The boys are on recess at the school next to where we're staying. They're playing soccer and volleyball; life must go on, and the children must be "carefully taught."

May 27 — on the ferry leaving Ireland

Last night's concert in Belfast will stay in my memory as long as I live.

Because of the curfew, the streets were empty when we arrived at what had once been a lovely old downtown theater. We were told that vehicles were not allowed to park on the streets unless attended by their drivers at all times.

The once-elegant old theater showed scars from the skirmishes it had seen. Plywood boards had been laid in the hallways to cover the places where the floor had been destroyed.

The eerie feeling of empty streets in a big city made me wary about the safety of the children, and I suspected that no one would show up for the concert because of the situation. But miraculously, from the darkness, people began to appear and file into that once-proud old building.

Guards with bulletproof vests stood sentinel at the stage door. The children stood beside them, and the concert started.

So many of our songs are about the oneness of believers—calling for unity in the Body of Christ, urging God's family to take the risk of loving across any barriers—that I feared they might be considered politically inflammatory in this city torn by factions and religious strife.

And we were tired, drained by an intense TV interview right before the concert and frustrated by some electrical problems in the building.

But as I said, the people came.

The local promotion person estimated the audience to be about 65 percent Protestant and about 35 percent Catholic. But as we began to sing—words like "I'm so glad I'm a part of the family of God" and "I am loved, I am loved; I can risk loving you, for the One who knows me best loves me most. . . . Won't you please take my hand; we are free to love each other; we are loved" and "The Church Triumphant is alive and well!"—something began to happen. By the time we had finished the concert and ended with a beautiful, spirit-hushed time of worship, there was truly a "sweet, sweet spirit in that place."

Finally, Bill said, "We've been singing for you all night. I'd like you to sing for us now. Take the hand of your neighbor, across aisles, all over this building, and sing together, 'Blest Be the Tie That Binds.'"

When a thousand Protestant and Catholic Irish voices began to rise as one and fill that room with what was not just a song, but a pledge of Christian love bigger than century-old disputes, there was no keeping back the tears. I shall never forget those Irish brogues rising to proclaim that, "the fellowship of kindred minds is like to that above."

There was a moment of silence. No one could speak for the beauty of it. Then, like an explosive that could not be held back, we all broke into "Get all excited; go tell everybody that Jesus Christ is King."

There was spontaneous dancing in the aisles and hugs all around. Joy. The joy of knowing that no matter what the agenda of this world's powers, God is still the sovereign Lord—and it is *His* agenda that will be played out in the end.

This morning we left at 6:30 A.M. for the ferry. The Irish countryside was cloaked in fog, but the sun lay just above trying to burn through. All this gave a Narnia effect to everything: cattle appearing suddenly out of the mist as we drove along, the hills and trees all heather green with golden promise barely hidden.

We had a fine breakfast on the boat, and some of us took a nap. The kids are having a good time and are widening, ever widening, their horizons.

Our time in Ireland helps me comprehend just how complex the situation there is. The only answer seems to be for all truly born-again believers to share a common unity in Jesus—Catholics and Protestants alike—and let their oneness in Him overshadow their differences and enlarge their capacities for love.

May 29 — driving across the U.K.

Everyone in these countries seems to live life on a miniature scale—economized, pared-down. They eat small—only what they need, buying in small, non-wasteful amounts. They live small—smaller rooms, smaller beds, frailer furniture. They drive small—no oversized cars, no oversized freeways, no oversized trips across oversized countries.

Everyone seems confined in his or her assigned stratum of society, careful not to step over invisible but well-defined boundaries, although there is a great deal of pushing and shoving on the horizontal plane.

One thing that is *not* undersized is history and tradition. It looms tall over everything and tends to keep strictly enforced the restrictive atmosphere and conventions.

I get the feeling that in spite of the very visible propriety of convention, however, there is seething underneath a decadent personal anarchy and permissiveness. I have the feeling that the standards of propriety should not be mistaken for morality or purity. There is a certain godlessness that seems to be deep in the heart of things, carefully covered by the deceptive armor of convention.

This society seems to have preserved and economized their material and natural resources very well, but have not paid as careful attention to their spiritual and moral resources.

We Americans can take both example and warning. We tend to throw away our material and natural resources. It remains as yet to be seen whether we are, as a society, throwing out our spiritual resources as well. Perhaps we have been generous, for instance, only out of our plenty. As material things dwindle, will we become grasping and miserly, or is our generosity a spiritual resource we will recognize and preserve? Have we been God-minded because our wealth has reminded us of our Creator, or has our plenty made gods of our own minds that we will worship more and more as we destroy the shrines of nature and replace them with shrines of technology?

May 30 — Sweden

The first concert in Sweden was very difficult. We worked through a translator who was not familiar with American idioms. The church was small, and we had to keep the volume very, very low. I did not feel they liked it much even then. Maybe tonight will be better.

I am having coffee in a small cafe in the hotel. A Spanish

waitress is helping here who speaks both English and Swedish. I feel no real barrier between her and myself. She is a woman. She makes coffee in the mornings, gets her children off to school, and tries to make ends meet at the market. She is very bright, her snapping eyes tell me. Yet she serves. She manages here in this restaurant. She is capable of more.

That is something women everywhere share in common. Perhaps that is why they can make do, be happy wherever they are; they're used to making contentment out of whatever comes—always making something from nothing, stretching the stew, remaking the worn-out clothes or opportunity into something "new" and presentable, smiling and caressing in spite of their own inclinations to tears and fatigue—mothering the world. Yet while their hands perform the familiar tasks, their minds race on—assimilating, analyzing, philosophizing.

Someone has said that men are "affective" while women are "reflective." That is probably true. So much of men's thinking is applied directly to their work. The result of their thinking is output, income, product. But most of what women think about does not affect the material world; indeed, their assigned roles prevent this. Their pondering is, instead, about the quality of life in an abstract sense, and too often is not considered very useful to making concrete products, unless one gives importance to people as a product—people who ask *why* they're alive. That's the industry of the heart.

May 31 — Sweden

The concert tonight was better and went more smoothly. It is difficult to maintain emotional intensity when working through an interpreter, but we are getting more comfortable with it.

The young people who know English like the concerts. They sort of apologize for the reserved reception given us by the adults.

Our children are adjusting very well. Amy picked up some phrases of Swedish today: "My name is Amy" and "Thank you very much." A few weeks and the kids would have built several spans of the bridge to another culture. Suzanne stayed in a Swedish home tonight.

I feel that every experience here is valuable and well worth the effort. It is good for *us* to be the minority, the disadvantaged, the misunderstood—if for no other reason than to show us the meaning of compassion and patience. We will reach farther as the result of this experience.

The country itself is beautiful, much like northern Michigan, with acres of birch, pine, and poplar. The houses are of wood, neat and simple, with tiled roofs, much like Michigan houses in the upper peninsula. My body-clock is still a bit off, but last night's sleep sure helped!

June 2 — Stockholm

I am sitting here beside the wide waters that divide this old city into islands. The shipping industry is going on around me. While the others are meeting about Swedish publishing, I have stolen away to this secluded spot on the banks of the fjord. I am still and aware of God's presence, the same familiar presence I know when I am quiet at home. Yes. God is here.

June 5 — Sweden

How can I describe Sweden? A country of contradictions. A people quiet, timid, and reserved on the one hand; loose and liberal on the other. A people who frown on lipstick, yet look with favor on nudity. A people who are sedate in church, yet import American rock music and export pornography. A people whose naturally gentle nature collides with the decaying moral climate so that the young resort to alcohol to sedate their consciences and bolster their bravado.

We are leaving just as we are beginning to understand. We drive across the countryside at five in the morning, yet find that the sun has begun his pilgrimage across the summer sky more than two hours ago. His warm rays draw a dreamlike mist from the fertile wheat fields, a mist that drapes the earth's face like a veil for a bride on her wedding day. Soon the passionate sun will burn through, and the mystery will be gone from the morning.

But just now the sun turns the spider webs on the farm fences into gossamer lace and is reflected in crimson on the ripples of the harbor. The rabbits and gulls are gleaning the fields, getting the cream of the morning crop while the brazen but lazy blackbirds sleep. The silent birches gather nectar from the morning for growth and strength. And the pines reach for the sun while they can. I reach for warmth, too, and home.

June 16 — home

If I thought about the last month—the tour, then the marathon of recording sessions—I would get dizzy. But we are finally at home for good—at least for awhile. Benjy has been fishing and swimming this week. He and his cousin, David, caught five fish yesterday. But when David got home, his pet rabbit was dead. He was so upset he couldn't play or eat at the picnic. We felt so sorry for him.

Amy had just gone through the same thing the day before with a little wood duck some neighborhood kids brought over from the park—she just cried and cried. But in spite of the inevitable sadness, I still think little creatures are worth the struggle . . . they teach children compassion and the frailty of life, if nothing else. No love given away is ever wasted!

Today I fished with Benjy all day in the rain. We put a piece of plastic over the picnic table and sat under it and just kept on fishing. The catfish started biting every time the rain started, so we couldn't quit!

Monday night after all our company left, Bill and I went to Indianapolis to have a taco and see a movie. Then we went to the cabin alone and spent the night. It was wonderful—just what my soul (and body) needed.

Bill's so good and I'm so lucky. When I see all the women who have to spend their lives pretending to be simple and stupid because their husbands can't handle an equal, I'm doubly thankful for a man with a healthy ego and some self-confidence who wants me to become all I can be. Besides, he's a great lover!

Sunday we leave for Nantucket. The kids are *so* excited! We all love the sea, and especially that place. There are so many memories there.

July 10 – Nantucket

This wonderful week has sped by too quickly. Last night we had a wiener roast on Dionnes Beach. Then we searched the water for little creatures and found dozens of hermit crabs and other kinds of sea life. That beach is certainly our favorite—so quiet, so secretive and promising, so romantic.

Benjy's, Amy's and Suzanne's profiles between the pink horizon and the quiet sea are frozen in my mind as if someone had stopped a movie projector to take a closer look at one frame—this frame . . . this moment.

Benjy, so innocent on the outer edge of childhood, all freckled and windblown with his sun-bleached hair and dancing eyes, his sturdy little body and wide, strong hands.

Amy, so straight and tall with her first "real hair-do"—excited, bubbling, expectant, and always optimistic. Always making peace and making do with whatever circumstances or people she has to work with.

Suzanne, poised on the path to womanhood, yet wise enough to keep her childhood's wide-eyed wonder and excitement over simple things. Protective, inventive, and loyal, with an eye for art and beauty; self-sufficient, yet needing to be loved and touched and protected, too.

I see their faces there between the sea and sky, barely children, yet hardly mature. I stand on tiptoe and try to hold this moment in my mind, for this visit to our precious island will be like no other. We've celebrated the happy days of childhood here on these beaches and watched the little footprints in the sand. And now we make this island our welcome mat for grownup days.

If I look closely down the beach, I can see the prints of tiny toddler feet grow bigger as they run along until they end right here in front of me—long and slim and almost the size of mine. Growing feet. Running feet. Feet I've held in my hand and counted "piggies." Feet I've scrubbed the mud and sand and grass stains from. Feet I've tied sneakers on—and stiff new Sunday shoes. Feet I've taught to pedal bikes and to roller-skate. Feet I've taught to paddle when they swim and hold "just so" in stirrups when riding horses, with toes pointed in and heels out. Feet that learned to go where I couldn't follow . . . up tall trees, down school hallways, on dates.

I've watched those feet take first steps, toddle, walk, skip, balance, kick footballs, run bases, march in parades, and dance pirouettes. And at every stage I've watched them leave the current footwear behind to run barefoot and free down these beloved beaches.

July 28 — home

Since I last wrote, Benjy has had his tenth birthday. That seems to be the most important event.

Oh, the Shah of Iran died, there was an earthquake in the Midwest, Mount St. Helens erupted again, and Reagan was nominated to run on the Republican ticket. Our company spent a week at the Christian Booksellers Associate convention; I worked on the book with Shirley Dobson and met with the publishers. Billy Carter's alliance with Libya was revealed, Chanel came out with a new fashion line for fall, and General Motors announced a new X-body economy car for 1981. But, as I said before, the most important event was Benjy's tenth birthday

Ten years we've had him here in our family. Ten years of hugs and kisses, scoldings and prayers. Ten years of puppet shows and fishing, Star Wars and Johnny West. Ten years of Nikes and Adidas, Toughskins and Izods. Ten years of potato chips and hot dogs, piano books and drumsticks, drawing paper and Elmer's glue. Hundreds of giggles, quarts of tears, cartons of Band-Aids, miles of bike rides, yards and yards of fishing line, three tennis rackets, gallons of orange juice, countless baseballs and mitts and bats, and thirty-six report cards.

I see him now, silhouetted straight and sturdy against the dusky summer sky, waiting for his giant sparkler to ignite so he can run across the yard poking holes in the darkness.

It takes a while, doesn't it? You never know exactly when the sparks will start to fly—just when your torch will start the burning on its own.

There it goes, Benjy! I can see your face light up right with the sparkler. I watch you give fire to someone else, then run together down the hillside making crazy, glorious circles in the air.

And just when is it that the lights go on to stay in little boys and they begin to give their special warmth to this cold world? When is the magic moment that they catch on for themselves? When will the sparks begin to fly and I know you're burning on your own?

I feel the time is near, and I want to keep you close here to the fires of home. But one day—I know it—you will not need these fires to ignite you. You'll make your own shining difference in this world. And you will go on lighting up the future long after Dad and I have flickered out. July boy, it brings us joy to watch you grow, to see you glow, and to know that you will *make a difference* in this dark world.

August 6 — home

This has been a delicious summer—so full of love and time for each other. Even our activities and commitments have been together, so that makes them invaluable in more than one way.

Amy's legs have grown four inches, I know. She is such a little lady—yet curious, observant, and thinking. She reads constantly and devours Nancy Drew, Mary Poppins, books on horses, and any kind of mystery. Benjy divides his days between Star Wars, swimming, and fishing. He is *always* thinking, and he hears melodies in his head all day long. The drums are his release for all that would otherwise stay bottled up inside. He is seething with potential.

Suzanne has become an adult with lots of little girl innocence and joy. She is wise and funny and full of insight. We are friends, and I'd as soon talk to her about life as anyone I know. It's so rewarding to see her think and act responsibly on her own and exhibit such strength as to make good choices for herself as well as influence for right the choices of others.

Bill and I are growing, too. Life is so different, when we *live* it, from the way we *view* it in others.

I feel scared and excited all the time. Anxious, inadequate, and timid about what lies ahead. Rewarded, encouraged, and pleased about the stage I've just passed through. Because of ever-widening horizons, I never feel as if I've arrived, and I'm always in water over my head—too curious and excited to stay where I'm comfortable, yet never quite adequate for going on.

My skin grows older and more wrinkled, and my body thickens and sags, but the same kid lives inside that has always been there. The only thing different is people's expectation of and reaction to me.

But children know the truth. They are the only ones who know people for what they really are, and until they are taught our society's prejudice for youth, physical beauty, and the affectations of affluence, they go on loving and accepting the fellow-child in us all. Bless them . . . "for of such is the kingdom of Heaven."

October 2 — the cabin

I came here to write on the "moments" book, but so far have written a song instead.

It's hard to work today because autumn is so persistent about getting my attention. The birds and squirrels are busy making provision for winter, the first fire of the season keeps flickering and crackling to catch my eye and ear, the beech trees keep whispering about changing into their new fall fashions of gold, and the chestnuts keep dropping to the ground, making their own disturbance.

Even the air refuses to be sedate and quiet, but keeps sneaking around the corner of the porch, breathing nippy puffs at the back of my neck, only to pretend stillness when I turn to catch it at its game. A splash of red catches my eye, too. A black-and-white woodpecker tips his head to me in hopes that I will leave my silly work and join the celebration in the woods.

So how can I waste this day writing about "moments" and keep my good conscience? Should I squander this moment now and make a mockery of my intentions?

October 16 — home

Whenever we have cinnamon rolls for breakfast there is always a scramble to claim the "middle one." Benjy had won several times in a row, Suzanne got a turn last time, and today it was Amy's turn for sure. While she was still getting ready, Benjy came sniffing around to discover that I had fixed rolls today.

"I get the middle one!" he sang.

"No," I said, "it's Amy's turn today."

"Let's play a trick on her, then," he suggested. "Let's not put any icing on hers and see what she says."

I went along with the joke and iced all but the middle roll, saving back a little bit of icing to quiet the uproar after she discovered that her roll was slighted. Everyone sat at the table except Amy, who had run back to the bathroom to plug in her curling iron. Finally, she slid into her seat, and Benjy said, "I'll pray!"—probably because he wanted to make sure the prayer was short.

"Amen!" he said, and we began passing the rolls, ready to burst into laughter the minute the fun began. Only it *didn't!* Amy took the middle roll, smiled sweetly, and took a sip of her milk. No fuss; no uproar, no shouts of "Hey! It's not fair; you guys got all the icing."

Finally, Benjy said loudly, "I'll take this one. It has lots of icing!" Still no response. Amy just started eating her roll and peaches and drinking her milk.

"Amy," I said at last. "Didn't you notice your roll has no icing?"

"Oh, it's all right, Mom," she said. "I don't mind. I just thought there wasn't enough to go around. It's OK."

Well, that was the end of the joke, but what a way to start the day! What a reminder that "love is never selfish; does not insist on its own way; love hardly ever notices when others do it wrong."*

Thanks!

*Paraphrased from Living Bible translation of 1 Corinthians 13:4–5.

November 28 — home

Thanksgiving was truly a thanks-filled day for me. The children are all well and strong, Aunt Lillie was here to celebrate her eighty-eighth birthday, George and Lela* are well and happy.

We were especially glad for the way Lela is feeling after almost losing her this summer. Her diet has straightened out her body chemistry and her blood pressure, and she seems happier and more contented than I ever remember. George is so good to me, to us all, and does so many little things that could easily be overlooked because of his quiet way.

Mary Ann and Donnie† were here with all four of their kids home at once. And Mother was here, too, looking so pretty, as she always does.

Before dinner Amy gave each person a grain of Indian corn, as we always do, partly to remind us that the first Thanksgiving was no feast such as we had but a meager, much-awaited harvest; and that the list of "what I'm thankful for" that the pilgrims recited contained things like "being alive" (because many were *not* alive after the first year) and "having the house finished" (which meant literally having hewn a cabin out of the wilderness) and "food to keep us through the winter" (when that meager harvest meant the difference between life and death).

As we stood in a circle before we prayed, we passed the little basket around, and as each of us put in our single seed of corn, we told what we were most grateful for that had occurred since we stood in this circle one year ago.

Every gift of thanks was precious to me. Aunt Lillie told us that she'd dreamed her son, Paul, had been in a terrible wreck, then she'd awakened to his phone call saying he was safe in Oklahoma and would be home the next day.

*Bill's mother and father.
†Bill's sister and her husband.

George reminded us of the families, four hundred of them, left homeless by the California fires, and of the hundreds stricken by the earthquake in Italy—and how thankful we should be for simple shelter, food, and each other. As we went around the circle, the tears of gratitude washed away any masks we might have been tempted to wear, and we openly embraced each other with our hearts.

I feel so blessed and so rich. My petty gripes seem to pale in the sunlight of God's infinite goodness. I want so much to always see clearly the real things in life . . . the children, Bill's love, nature, the infinite variety in people, the moments I have, the talents I have to use. Blessed! I am so blessed—and so responsible!

1981

I see in mature faces the eyes of little boys....
And it sometimes scares me to know that the decisions
that affect the destiny of our galaxy
are being made by boys who haven't been touched in years....

January 18 — home

In December I hurried to finish all the preparations for Christmas before leaving for ten days in Israel. We had a wonderful and enlightening time. The Christmas story seemed so alive to us after having seen so much and felt so much of the land.

And it *is* the Land. It's as if the Land is the main character of Israel. One is always aware of its presence and its importance, like some powerful godfather that is both protection and protected. It is the Land that sustains, and it is the Land that must be preserved and defended.

Christmas was so relaxed and refreshing. Having all the work done so far in advance, then going away to a country where the celebration of Christmas is not felt or seen, then returning to our home, our family, and our festivities made everything more important and new.

So far in January about all we've accomplished is getting through the flu. Amy had it first, then Benjy and I. We have really had a hard time getting over it; it just seems to hang on and on.

One plus. I got to spend time alone with each of the children, just being together. It is good to just be lazy together once in a while.

It seems that all the negative things in almost any relationship can be fixed by spending quality time together without outside pressures. And quality time takes time.

I hear people say, "It's not the quantity of time that's important; it's the quality." Well, technically, that may be true, but quality doesn't happen in a hurry. There has to be time to waste, to settle in, to get comfortable, to let talk happen without pressure—time to get bored enough to turn to each other for stimulation. There has to be time to let each person see the other as the best, maybe the only, option for joy and sharing. No television, no parties or friends. No mechanical diversions. Just each other.

March 9 — home

Bill gave me a wedding ring. One night at supper he came in
looking as if he had something on his mind. He sat while
everyone got into their places and blessing was asked. Then
he said, "Everybody be quiet! I have a presentation!"

He handed me a tiny box. Inside was a beautiful gold band with
strange-looking figures embossed around it.

"I had it made in Israel," he said. "It says, 'Come away, my love'
in Hebrew."

I couldn't believe it. Amy said, "Oh, Daddy! That's so romantic! I
didn't know you could be so romantic!"

Bill had thought of it all by himself and had ordered it in
December when we were in Israel. The ring I'd been wearing I'd
bought myself about sixteen years ago at K-Mart while Bill was
looking at records. He'd always disliked the diamond set he got
when we were married, so that night for $13.95 I had bought the
plain gold band I'd worn ever since.

I think this is the sweetest thing Bill's ever done. It's so much
more than the gold or the ring. It's that he thought of it, planned
it, waited for it, and wanted it to mean something special.

1 9 8 1

Someday one of us will leave this world, probably ahead of the other. Whichever is left will keep this ring as a reminder that someone is waiting and longing and whispering, "Come away, my love. The winter is over. Flowers appear and springtime is coming—arise, and come away. . . ."*

And for now, I will look at it sometimes and know that, in the chaos of our schedule, our commitment to each other is telling us, "You need some time alone . . . you need to get away." And when we're apart, I'll know there's someone who loves me, whose thoughts are pulling me back to him with the message of the heart: "Come away, my love . . . come away."

March 10 — the cabin

The spring tour starts this week. It's a long one, so in a way I dread it, but we're excited, too, about some of the things we have to say.

This week, Bill's uncle Howard Hartwell came out and taught Bill and the kids how to tap maple trees. We have four taps now and are having fun collecting the sap. When I get back from the trip, we'll boil it down. I think they will always remember this experience. The cabin is so full of wonderful memories. I hope no other kind are ever made here. We must pledge to each other to keep it that way.

March 13 — on the road (spring tour)

Ready or not, we're back on the road. It's interesting how each thing we're called on to do is exciting in its own way—when the time comes. Always there's the element of stark terror, too,

*Song of Solomon 2:10–12, paraphrased.

at having tackled a job too big for our abilities, but that is the challenge and, in the end, the joy.

Because of expenses and the economy, we have cut back this trip—fewer people and almost no flying. We rented an extra bus, which for me is preferable to flying. I enjoy the time to think and read.

I will miss the children; I always do when we're gone for more than two days. I think it is good for them to learn to manage and operate without us, to make good decisions and to care for each other. It's probably good, too, for Bill and me to have some time together without them, to be with each other away from the pressures of home and office.

All the same, I'll miss them and will get homesick for routine. But they will leave with us and travel a couple of days before returning to school. I will savor these days.

April 2 — on the road

More than a week since I wrote. Concerts have been very exciting, and we all feel it's the strongest program yet. We went home after Macon, Georgia, and brought the kids back with us. They are on spring vacation this week, so it's been fun having them along.

This trip will be historical for us all. We were in Washington, D.C. on Monday. Our friend, Lou Gerig, who is with the White House Press Corps, had made arrangements for us to see the Oval Office and the Cabinet Room while President Reagan was gone making a speech at the Washington Hilton.

We were laughing about the huge jar of jelly beans on the cabinet table when everyone started running back and forth and said we'd have to hurry out. They said the President was on his way back. We went down to the gate to see Reagan's car come in, but it never came.

Finally, we walked back to Lou's office. His secretary was on the phone and the TV was reporting something about an incident at the Washington Hilton. The assistant who was with us asked her what was going on. She looked stricken and said, "Here's what I was just told on the phone." Then she wrote on a piece of paper and handed it to the assistant. By now the TV was showing that three men had been shot—one of whom was Jim Brady, Lou's boss.

The secretaries were very upset; some cried. Lou had been summoned to the White House to cover in Brady's absence, since the others in the Press Corps were with Brady at the hospital.

At first they said the President had not been injured, but later they said that he had been—a bullet had entered just under his left ribs when he raised his arm to wave. Two other men had been shot, too. The assailant had been immediately apprehended—a young man named John Hinckley.

We watched it all in Lou's office. When we learned that Lou would not be returning, we took a cab in the rain to a deserted restaurant and ate and talked about what one says and sings at a concert when the whole nation is in shock.

By concert time, the news that the President had returned from surgery in excellent condition was well known, the other three men were all alive, and the assailant had been arraigned.

The people came in an attitude of relief and thanksgiving, the presence of the Holy Spirit made the "family" awareness very real, and the whole evening was a gift of celebration as well as a time of realigning priorities. We all realized anew how fragile life can be and how much we should focus on important things.

After packing up equipment, we drove on to Hempstead, N.Y. and from there to Harrisburg, Pennsylvania. Only three more days, and we'll be done 'til fall!

April 26 — home

The experiences of the trip left us all changed, made us grow, but the best thing of all is coming home. Even in the middle of the night when we got in from Dayton, I could see that the daffodils were in bloom. Spring was "happening."

This week we have just basked in "homeness." There's been

much fresh rain and the buds are bursting out all over. The hillsides are green, green, while the weeping willows are yellow, yellow. Birds and squirrels are busy everywhere, and the sap is running so strongly that one can almost hear it in the trees.

We're thinking about a praise and worship album. It's a lovely time to write for it because praise fills our hearts. This is a day that the Lord has made. We *will* rejoice and be glad in it.

May 7 — home

I am struggling with this book on decision-making: it is moving along quite well, but the problem is with examples and illustrations.

So many of the things in our lives that have taught us the principles of decision making, I can't tell because they involve other people in our public lives.

The other personal things are too positive. It might sound as if we've never made mistakes. The truth is, Bill and I have done a few things right, but I have a feeling people would rather hear about our failures than our good choices. We have tried to depend daily on the Lord, and He has helped and preserved us time and time again.

How can I explain building this cabin eight miles from home so that we can absorb nature and have a plan for listening? How do I tell that Bill spends his life protecting us from the public that we at the same time love and serve? How do I tell that he's had the good sense to recognize that if we let the public eat us alive, we will have nothing of value left to give them? How do I write how thankful we are for the children, for their sweet attitudes and personal lifestyles? How do I rejoice, humbly as I feel, in the richness of their gifts to us of love and respect and service?

I saw a yellow wild canary (finch) today. The woods are turning green and the meadow across the creek is slowly being hidden by the foliage. The wild cherries and dogwood wave their white flags through the deepening green. The things I ordered to plant came yesterday, so I'll need to quit writing to get them into the ground after school.

May 20 — home

Yesterday I went out to have lunch with Benjy at school. He was working—punching meal tickets for the cafeteria. I watched him and waited until everyone was through the line so we could eat together. I talked to all of his friends—so many little boys that he has brought home at some time or another.

After lunch, Benjy wanted me to see the space mural he'd been working on. He's a pretty good artist, so he'd been chosen again to make the mural for his classroom. He was pleased.

I felt sad as I left. I knew this was probably the last time I'd ever go to the elementary school to have lunch with one of our children. Benjy—the last one—will leave in a few more days.

It seems like only yesterday that I drove him there his first day of kindergarten with his box of Kleenex, his school box, and his new blue-and-white tennis shoes.

He was so confident that day, although there have been some not-so-confident days since—like the day he found out he hadn't made the basketball team and the day he got his first bad grade on a paper.

But there have been days that confirmed his value to himself—the day he played the *long* song he had written on the piano for PTA and the day he was chosen to be in charge of the art project and his first time to make three home runs in one kickball game.

What I knew that first day was indeed true—children are never quite the same after they start school. But the change in him has made us proud. He is becoming . . . one step at a time.

June 8 — the cabin

We brought Benjy and Amy and three of the cousins out here to the cabin last night to stay. The kids collected kindling and made a bonfire when we got here. Then they roasted marshmallows and sat by the fire.

It's cool and fragrant out here. We've seen lots of deer tracks—some big ones—and raccoon. The stream is high from all the rain, and everything is very green.

The trees seem to have their own personalities and character. My favorite is the reassuring basswood that I'm sure once spread its lovely umbrella of protection over the Indian maidens as they wove their cloth or patted out corn cakes beside the laughing brook. And here am I, making bran muffins and mending the broken string on Benjy's bow. Not so different are we. While our culture brags "progress" and "liberation," the basswood knows which of us is most advanced and free.

And deep inside I know, too. The depths of me long to run to the woods and think of ageless things beside the stream when work is done and the little braves have gone off in search of adventure. And since the Indian maidens are gone, I ask the abiding basswood to whisper its timeless secrets to me. It stands there with its tidy bark and substantial twin trunks that look like the sturdy legs of some prehistoric mammoth. I listen.

There are other trees to talk to: the dogwood and the maple. But when I sit beside the basswood and the oak, I listen.

July 23 — home

Benjy is at basketball camp this week. It seems as if the bottom has dropped out of our family without him. He sounds so small when he calls on the phone—not at all boisterous and confident as he does at home. All the bravado is gone, and all that's left is his real self, vulnerable and childlike.

Some boys gave him a hard time the second day, caught him between activities, threatened and harassed him and his friend and talked filthy to them. We were all upset. He is so innocent as yet, and it is important for him to remain so as long as possible.

When he called to tell us, he said, "Mom, it's goin' bad; it's all goin' bad."

"What's goin' bad?" I asked.

"Oh, not basketball camp. That's good! And the coach is good. It's the kids. The kids are goin' bad."

How I love him and hurt for him! I wish I could take for him the evil he will face and save him from it. It makes me angry that little boys and girls even have to be made aware and wary of things like filthy language, homosexuality, abuse, and the like before their emotions have time to mature.

But we have no choice. The likelihood of a bad experience is great enough that to have them unprepared might cause irreparable damage. It seems that, along with natural resources and simple lifestyles, even childhood is being eroded away. Human beings are forced to go from infancy to adolescence with no joy years.

Well, I went over to camp today to see Benjy. He seems to be

doing quite well now and seems happy. But he seems a little older
and a little more serious. Manhood is beginning to ripple under
the muscles of his strong little shoulders. He's lost weight and
slimmed down. He lifted his shirt to show me his flat tummy. The
muscles of his legs have hardened and slimmed. But deep in his
eyes is the same timid little boy who is apprehensive of the first
day of school and who wakes sometimes with bad dreams and
needs to be held.

I see boys in eyes everywhere . . . boys in prison, boys in the
Pentagon, boys in management, and boys in the battlefield mud.
From newspaper clippings and television coverage, from behind
massive mahogany desks and behind pulpits, I see in mature faces
the eyes of little boys. Boys who are unsure and hurt and afraid.
Boys who need to be encouraged, reassured, and held. And it
sometimes scares me to know that the decisions that affect the
destiny of our galaxy are being made by boys who haven't been
touched in years.

September 11 — home

Beautiful fall day—warm and fragrant, the air laden with the
smells of harvest time: the scent of grain and grasses freshly
cut, the pungent smells of apples and peaches, the musty smell
of the damp, freshly plowed earth, the nutty smell of acorns
and buckeyes.

There is a delicious melancholy in the wind, a whispered
knowing that these days are numbered and the countdown to
winter is nearing zero.

This time of year makes me want to save something—peaches,
apples, nuts, and moments—or to fix something—the broken
yard swing, a wear-worn room, neglected relationships. I feel an
urgency to take advantage of every sunrise.

Last night we gathered up what we could find and had a picnic
at Mounds Park with the Guillen family. It was a perfect evening.
We grilled hamburgers, then played a few innings of kickball.
By then it was almost dark, so we took a lantern and walked
the trails.

Benjy ran ahead and hid in the shadows so he could jump out
and scare us. Amy and David Guillen teetered on the edge between
childhood friendship and adolescent attraction. Some
of us stayed close to Mother so she could negotiate the root-infested
path and the sharp inclines with her disintegrating knees.

When we got back to our picnic site, the coals were still
glowing. We had some watermelon and watched the almost-full
moon. Benjy and I went over in the clearing to sit on a stump. We
talked about his class and reminisced about the trip we'd taken to
the park in the spring.

He said one of his friends at school was "going with" a girl.
When I asked who he was "going with," he said, "Nobody. Do you
think I should go with somebody?"

"I don't know," I answered, "You have a lot of neat friends in
Nashville and other places. You might not want to tie yourself
down to anybody. Just maybe be friends to everybody."

"Yeah," he said, as if that was what he'd already decided. "But I wouldn't mind going with a girl sometime."

We watched the moon, listened to the crickets, then went back to meet the others to pack the supplies in the cars for the trip home.

What a stroke! To steal that experience right out from under the nose of the advancing calendar.

September 25 — fall tour

Jackson, Dallas, Houston . . . for me, not places with names, but items on the itinerary that mark the space between my leaving and my returning home.

The places march along, carrying me farther and farther away until the midpoint, where we turn around and start measuring our way back again. Still on our ascent, we climb to the pinnacle as home fades gradually into the mist of remembered moments in my mind. Nostalgia moves in to replace the tangible "now," and I shift into the mental processes that keep me suspended between the points of return. . . .

September 27 — on the road

I woke this morning at a truck stop in west Texas . . . nothing for miles but sagebrush and cacti, roadrunners and rattlesnakes. Truckers were pulling their rigs in from all-night drives through the desert to swap road tales and pocketknives and women.

In the restroom I met one well-traded woman who seemed to have not been a person for a long time—at least three years, she told us, that being the length of time she'd been the property of her current "love." Misused and seemingly abandoned, she fought back the tears as she struggled with the prospects of her immediate future. I am haunted by the knowing that I left her there without a single lifeline.

Just past noon we are nearing El Paso. The flatlands have bulged into rocky hills, and the smoky sage has been colored by yellow clumps that look like mustard. Yucca plants hold tenaciously to the rocky slopes. Now and then there is a clapboard shack baking in the Texas heat—just the kind that inspired Steinbeck's stories of hard times in the "bad lands."

We keep reminding Gary of what we saved him from! Yet there is a kind of sober and stark beauty here. I am constantly amazed at the variety of God's creative work. Each part of the world seems to have its own special uniqueness that is somehow right with living things that are happy right where they are.

Mesquite trees and sagebrush could not survive in Indiana, nor could corn and sycamores live here. Yet the spectrum of blues and grays are as delicate and subtle as the greens and golds are beautiful and bright.

Yes!

October 1 — on the road

I find I have to put my mind in some special kind of neutral to stay away this long. Long absence throws all my natural chemistry off.

The concerts have been excellent, but it is hard to keep enough of my heart here to be complete between concerts. It becomes a circus existence: get up, eat breakfast, read, take a bath, go to early supper, sound check, get ready, do the concert, talk to people, get into the bus, drive all night, and start again.

Interspersed are some lovely moments with the troupe, and often there are wonderful times with Bill. But somehow it all takes on an aura of fantasy—like riding a glider, looking for a safe and solid place to land.

I've even taken up embroidery, would you believe! I'd rather write, but the bus is too bumpy, and my creative energies are drained by the intense exertion of the concerts and the dulling boredom of endless miles.

I would love the miles if there were time to stop and see things, but we're always driven right past the wonders of the world by the tyranny of our schedule. I've been in every state in the Union, yet I've never seen the Grand Canyon, Yellowstone, Yosemite, the Tetons, Glacier National Park, a Black Hills passion play, or the islands in Puget Sound.

But I've seen people—and the terrains that mold their temperaments and shape their values. I've sensed the demands made on them by their stubborn rocks or the severity of their climates. I've seen the barren deserts that threaten them and the crowded cities that rob them of their personal uniqueness. I've seen the wide-open spaces that teach them to trust other human beings, and I've seen the congested neighborhoods that teach them to grab and hold and peer at the world through frightened eyes and cynical mindsets.

I've touched the children—from Manhattan to Montana, from San Antonio to Saginaw—and I've felt the hope and fear in them.

I've watched them reach for me in open affection and shrink from me in fearful distrust. I've seen promises with blond pigtails and black shiny pixies. I've had black and brown, yellow, white, and reddish arms around my neck. With my heart I've learned to understand love in a dozen languages.

I've heard their parents say, "come to us!" They say it from the unknown seclusion of North Dakota. They say it from the anonymity of the Bronx. They say it from the mountain poverty of Kentucky and from the lighted plastic glitter of Las Vegas.

"Come to us!" they say. "Don't forget us."

As if we could.

"Why do you do it?" the glib reporters ask. I find myself looking into their eyes for some clue to the living person inside the professional—only a person could understand. Otherwise, I don't have the words. I'm sure they'd smile their well-rehearsed, objective, detached smiles and be polite while I say, "It's Jesus. He's come to us and given us life. Now we have to go."

They'd nod politely and think "money," "glamour," "travel," "fame," "excitement." They'd only think it was a gimmick if I told them that my mother's heart is pulled apart, my body is exhausted, and my brain is in suspension. They wouldn't believe me if I told them it's the Reason bigger than life, the Place wider than here, the Time beyond the now, and the unforgettable voices rising over millions of miles and fifteen years of days, joining in a deafening chorus that will not go away, "Come to us. Don't forget us!"

. . . And I know I have to go because Someone came to me.*

October 5 – Butte, Montana

Woke up here to beautiful snow-capped mountains and crisp, nippy air. This lazy copper-mining town seems to be caught in a lovely time warp, its people content to stay.

We've had several things go wrong with the vehicles this trip—two tires went out on the crew bus last week, the truck ran out of gas one night, another tire had to be bought, and last night the governor on the other bus went out in the mountains.

Otherwise, the trip has been smooth and very satisfying. The chemistry is very good among all the people on staff, and the spirit has been positive.

I miss the kids. Bill called home from the airport last night. Benjy was still awake (11:00 P.M. at home) and wanted to talk to me. Bill said I was on the plane. Benjy said, "Well, we're not homesick or anything—just come on home, okay?"

*This piece in 1987 actually became the inspiration for the lyric, "We Have Seen the Children."

October 9 — Seattle, Washington

I said the drive from Butte to Great Falls was beautiful . . . well, the drive from Spokane to Seattle has it beat! The Cascade Mountains, the wide river gorges, waterfalls cutting silver ribbons through the green-black, fir-covered hillsides, the highway winding through the narrow passes. And then the ocean! My soul settles in at the sight of the sea!

Sea gulls and ships, the smell of fishermen's nets drying in the sun, the mist moving like a lady in her chiffon evening gown across the harbor . . . something special to welcome all the senses, something to remind us that the act of creation which preceded us all was the "let it be" that moved across the face of the deep and brought the very ground of our beginnings from the waters.

I'm reading Lewis and Clark's journal. What an expedition *that* must have been—up the Missouri all the way to the sea through virgin land! I suppose during that fall the hillsides were a riot of color as they are today. It's hard to imagine this beauty with no traffic, no railroads, no power lines, no foresters' saws, no cities, and no industry. Glorious!

October 13 — on the road

Woke at the Husky Truck Stop in Rock Springs, Wyoming. Had some biscuits and eggs so that Ron, who was driving, could sleep an hour or so. Bill and I and several others talked and took our time over cups of hot truck-stop coffee.

A weather-worn man in an army snowsuit came in from the trail with his backpack; he was talking to himself and fell asleep over his cigarette and coffee. He'd been crossing this wasteland on foot and obviously came in to get warm.

It's a rugged life out here. Snow in the passes already. Shale caverns and rolling wilderness are dotted here and there with an oil company's trailer park and wells. That's about the only signs of life—with the exception of giant hawks and rattlesnakes.

I keep thinking of my grandparents, who came here by covered wagon with a baby all the way from Missouri, traveling across Nebraska to homestead in Wyoming. What a desolate place it must have been! Where did they get supplies? What happened when the baby got sick—or when the next one was born? No wonder Grandma was such a tough, self-made woman who could fix, make, or doctor anything.

Stopped to sleep in Kearney, Nebraska. Ron had been driving for about twenty hours. Nice, clean motel and good rates.

Had a good night's rest and breakfast. Sleep and nourishment are two of God's greatest gifts! No matter how tired we are or how big the problems seem, energies are restored in the morning! I can never remember a day in my life when I wasn't glad to see the morning. There have been days that I knew held difficult times, but I've never not wanted to face the day.

I love the dawn in any form: the dark mornings of winter, special made for building kitchen fires to warm little bodies and hearts; the expectant mornings of spring, with the birds announcing the sunrise an hour before the day breaks; the warm, lazy mornings of summer, when no matter how early I rise, dawn is always way ahead of me; the cool, sad mornings of autumn, with the air filled with the smell of grapes from the arbor and chrysanthemums and the smoke from burning leaves and the first wood fires.

Always new. Always exciting. Always full of promise. The mornings of my life, each my personal daily miracle!

October 15 — Normal, Illinois

THE KIDS ARE COMING TONIGHT! Should be in around seven o'clock. We've missed them so.

The concerts have been good every night and the audiences receptive. I feel the value of what we do. But I'm tired, homesick, and longing to have our family together again.

To know the fall is happening every day in Indiana and that we're not there to see it makes me sensitive to the passing moments. I wonder if the two hard maples by the driveway at home are as glorious as they've been other years. They change late, so maybe we'll get back in time to see them yet.

October 17 — Tulsa, Oklahoma

Two more concerts. Every time I begin to feel that there just isn't another one in me, I end up knowing that there was one more . . . in Him.

October 24 — home

Finally, things are returning to normal after our long, long tour. The tour was probably the best yet, and the tour group chemistry was good. The stories that keep coming in from the concerts are almost more than we can handle. I guess if we thought about the problems and heartaches represented in an audience, we wouldn't be able to even go out there. But the Lord seems to always take what we have to give and add to it to make available what the people need.

The kids are settling back in their normal groove, and so am I. I couldn't wait to build a fire in the kitchen, bake some pumpkin pies, and tuck the kids into their own beds at night. Life is so good and rich, I feel I have to grab every moment I possibly can.

How I love this fall. The leaves were a riot of color when we got home, and everything is dancing its loveliest swan song. The mums and marigolds are blooming their little lives away, and the birds are beginning to come closer in search of food.

1982

Even blindfolded I would recognize the specialness of this moment, and I see it with such focus that I almost have to turn my eyes away.

March 5 — home

I'm forty. I don't feel forty. Strange how your body fools people on the outside into thinking you are somehow changing, becoming one of society's stereotypes—an "adolescent," a "single adult," a "college student," a "middle-aged woman," a "senior citizen" or "golden ager"—while all along you stay the same.

I want to shout out from behind the fictitious facade, "Hey! It's me! The kid who used to lose her skate key in the cracks of the sidewalk, the girl who treasured her gray felt skirt with the seed pearl trim and turned her hair under in a pageboy.

"It's me—the one who panicked when there was a timed test in typing class, yet thrived on composition writing deadlines. Remember me? I'm the one who went stone dead just before the wedding march and resurrected with the kiss.

"I haven't changed. I'm still uncertain, nervous, insecure, and hesitant. I'm also confident, independent, adventuresome, and calm in a crisis.

"My body's playing a trick on us both—you out there and me in here. It looks to us both as if I am a mature, middle-aged woman, but I'm a beginner, a dreamer, a hoper, a schemer—a child, a girl, a woman—and I'm alive in here!"

It won't be long until tour. I both dread it and look forward to it. I hate leaving the kids; I love being with Bill. I dread coming to grips again with my failures as a musician and singer; I look forward to communicating God's love and mine to real people. I look forward to the empty days that I can fill with reading, writing, and relationships; I dread the fantasy of the circus life.

Yet, I commit once more to it all—for better or worse—and know that it is ordered by the One who knows me best and loves me most.

We got more snow this week, but most of it melted. I'm really sick of winter. It's been one of the longest ones I can remember, but that may be good. Perhaps the flowers and fruit blossoms won't come out too early, only to be damaged by a late freeze. The brook sounds wonderful today because of the thaw, and the birds are singing hesitantly.

May 14 — home

Tour is over, the kids are anxious for school to be out, and we're all trying to soak up every minute we can of summer. I've been planting flowers and digging in the dirt; Bill's been coming home at noon to get some sun.

The tour was good and there were several memorable moments. Bill and I had a good time together, too, and the children seemed to do well at home. When we got home, there was a huge yellow and red banner across the grape arbor that said, "WELCOME HOME MOM & DAD." Another sign was on the back door: "IT IS FINISHED; the tour is over!"

It was about ten in the morning on Mother's Day when we got there, so the kids were having their own church service. Benjy had just chosen as his scripture, "Don't be involved in silly controversy; don't argue!"* When he read it, he stopped to give Amy a meaningful stare.

When we got in they all had Mother's Day cards and gifts. Suzanne had a lovely potted mum; Amy had some nice perfume. Benjy had made his card himself by cutting letters out of the newspaper. The letters said, "Latest Headline: The Greatest Mother in the World." Then inside it read, "Gloria Gaither." And then there was a poem in red magic marker:

> Roses are red
> Violets are blue;
> My Mom's the best
> And she's pretty too.

On the back was this postscript:

> P.S. I have a surprise for you.
> Love, Benjy.

As soon as I read it, he grabbed my hand and pulled me out the door and to the garage. Even though I'd been on the bus all night and looked like death warmed over, he told me to get on my bike and follow him. Together we rode through the neighborhood and ended up at DeVaney's Bait Shop. He had evidently talked Bill DeVaney into opening his shop early on Sunday. Benj stopped beside a huge fish tank, pointed to an eighteen-inch largemouth bass and said proudly, "Happy Mother's Day! Do you like it?"

Well, what could I say? And anyway, before I could answer he interrupted excitedly, "Well, I thought and thought what would make you happiest for Mother's Day, and I knew nothing would make you more happy than seeing my bass! I caught him yesterday!"

And I was happy. I had a very creative son, and I was probably the only mother in America who got a live largemouth bass for Mother's Day!

---

*2 Timothy 2:23, paraphrased.

June 21 — the cabin

Benjy is in Nashville; he stayed there when we went down last week to work on our Christmas album and tape a TV commercial. Ronn Huff took him to the farm for the weekend and then he was going to be the deejay for Shana MacKenzie's neighborhood disco on Monday.

Suzanne is at Girl's State—we took her yesterday afternoon and left her in that big old dorm on the Indiana State campus in Terre Haute. She didn't know anyone, and she seemed so small and alone when we left her. It will be a good experience for her to have to find a way to reach out and relate, but we missed her before we even got out of the driveway. (She called this morning to say that she is homesick.)

When we got home, the house seemed empty and haunted by little voices with both Suzanne and Benjy gone, so Amy and I got up at 5:45 this morning and came to the cabin to write and think. We were out here by 6:30, fixed some sausages and blueberry muffins, and went for a walk in the wet, dewy field. Then we read Trina Paulia's *Hope for the Flowers* and a bit from Henry Nouwen's *Open Hands* about silence and how our culture is foreign to it.

Around 8:00, Bill came out and brought Carman. What a great young man he seems to be, so sensitive and committed. We wrote some songs, mostly music to lyrics I already had—"He Can Be Touched," "His Name Is Yaweh"—and then I wrote verses to the chorus Carman and Bill wrote last time he was here. It's called, "His Name Is Life." There were a few interruptions, but we had a great morning. Amy wrote a story about a spider and had the thrill of being consumed by inspiration. The ideas were coming to her so fast her pen could hardly keep up.

Bill invited the Weimers and the Malbones over for a cookout later. It was a perfect day—cool and lovely, the earth freshly washed with rain and the breeze gentle. We ended up sitting around the campfire until 10:00 P.M. and singing together—all the grownups and the children. Then we prayed together and brought

the picnic things up in the wagon to the house. We missed
Suzanne and Benjy, though, and are eager for them to come home.

June 22 — home

Bill and I stayed at the cabin overnight while Amy stayed with
the Malbones. Carman came out again this morning and
wrote the chorus of a song we'll call "He Walks Beside Me,
and I Am Not Afraid."

Suzanne called again to say she's lonely and homesick. I'd like
to go get her, but they don't want them to leave once they agree
to go. She said her stomach was upset and she had broken out in
a rash. I don't know if all that is good for her or not. It is an honor
to be chosen, but she would be happier if she knew someone she
felt comfortable with.

Today is Amy's thirteenth birthday—a teenager. She has
been a total delight and is becoming something very special, as
we always knew she would. I pray for her often as she sleeps,
that not one bit of her potential will be wasted—her joy, her flair
for drama, her spiritual sensitivity, her instinct for comforting
the hurting. We'll have a party tonight—she wants a wiener roast
with family and friends.

Where has the summer gone? June is nearly over, and I still haven't had a chance to be lazy.

June 29 — at the cabin

Amy is still in Michigan with Mother, and I miss her so. Funny how one child cannot take another's place. Missed Suzanne all last week and Benjy before that. Things don't seem right until all three are tucked into their own beds and filling their own places at the table.

Suzanne made it through the week at Girl's State, and I guess the experience was good for her, but she was so glad to get home. I made some fresh strawberry ice cream, and then we all went for a convertible ride.

Saturday night Bill and I took Benjy and went to Cicero fishing. We took our supper in the cooler and rented the last boat they had. The oars didn't fit right, and the crazy thing was impossible to row. Bill got motion sickness because it was too tippy.

We decided we should find someone who'd be interested in going in with us on a boat that is big enough to float with some stability. Maybe next summer we'll do that. Anyway, we had fun and the night was beautiful. Benjy was patient with us as we tried to keep up with his fishing skill. Bill got his line caught twice, but none of us caught any fish!

I long for some time to get alone out here to think and experiment with some ideas I have. I'd like to write for joy, not for any particular project—to have time really to ponder the goodness of God and how blessed I am. I go about my days knowing it, aware of it, yet for my gratitude to reach the plateau of a sacrifice of praise, I must ponder it, give time to it, give my praise substance.

So many have said that the highest praise is not thoughts or words but deeds, and I guess that's true enough. But in my life I feel so pressured to produce, to act, to create some tangible expression that will reach or touch others—something practical, functional, usable.

Sometimes I feel a deep longing to give my best time and energies to God alone in a way that will produce nothing tangible or visible. I long to confirm for myself the suspicion that He would be pleased for me to "waste" some time and energy and words (by the world's standards—even the "stewardship" oriented Christian world's standards) and with extravagance and abandonment lavish all my love on Him.

I'd like to write for no other reason, to spill the expensive essence of my best ideas on His feet and never count the cost, oblivious to those around me who would rather see it printed and shrink-wrapped, bottled in pretty vials, and sold to feed the poor.*

July 7 – home

With cascades of fire and stars we have celebrated our liberty and this nation's independence. And for one joyous weekend we have put from our national minds our ominous dependence on the volatile Middle East for life-sustaining energy and on the other unstable nations of the world for not lighting the fuse of world conflagration that would end all liberty forever.

Last night we went to some friends' for supper and had a little incident with Suzanne. On the surface it involved her leaving the party early. But more accurately it involved her parents' struggle with the difficult task of letting go of a once-little girl who is now a young adult, ready and capable of making some choices of her own. She is a great kid and is making good moves, but it is still hard to do things as a family without her and learn to enjoy them.

Being a parent is as crazy and unpredictable as being a growing child, and the adjustments are just as unprecedented and

*This journal entry later became the basis for the song, "Broken and Spilled Out."

difficult. There *must* be eternity—this life is all training ground for something!

I just hope our kids are patient with us as we learn how to parent, and I hope God helps us to be patient with them as they learn to be people.

July 23 — home

Benjy had a birthday this week—his twelfth—with his friends and the whole family here for a wiener roast to celebrate.

Jamie Heiser brought him a new fish for his aquarium, Davy Huff gave him a new rocket to build, and we got the electric guitar he's been so eager for. He had a great time opening presents and thanked each person—without being told. He definitely seemed older—more gentle, more self-controlled, yet still excited and childlike in so many ways. I hope he never outgrows that—his sense of joy and wonder.

Twelve: half-man, half-boy. One minute trying to fold up his legs enough to fit on my lap and the next wanting to go without us to the 4-H fair with his cousins. Wanting to wear the same old comfortable shirt for three days in a row, yet standing for hours to make sure his hair is just right. Working through his thought processes, shaping his own values, learning to stand alone when he needs to. Man—boy—with a heart as tender as a day-old bean sprout, a temper as quick and as unpredictable as an Indiana springtime thunderstorm, a grin as wide and as warm as a July sunset, and enough energy to solve the power shortage.

What a gift! What a trust! What a joy!—little twelve-year-old boy!

August 26 — home

(To Suzanne:)

School didn't start until one o'clock, so there was plenty of time for breakfast at McDonald's and shopping for the supplies that had been listed in the *Times Tribune* the Wednesday before. It was you who reminded us to go to McDonald's for breakfast. "We always have—the first day of school," you said.

Something hard to label stirred inside me when you said it. Perhaps it was pride—pride that you still found joy in our crazy little tradition. And perhaps it was pleasure—pleasure in knowing that you still choose to be with our family when you have your "druthers." But there was a certain sadness, too, and I couldn't stop the knowing that this was your last first day of school.

You came down the stairs that morning all neat and well-groomed, the healthy glow of your summer tan and freckles still showing through your make-up. your sun-bleached hair carefully arranged. "Hi, Mom!" you said, and your grin showed your straight, white teeth. *No more orthodontist appointments*, I thought, *and no more broken glasses to glue before school.* Contacts and braces had sure been worth it.

"I've got to have my senior pictures taken tomorrow after school, Mom. Can I use the car?"

"As far as I know," I answered. then reminded you of your promise to take your sister to get her hair trimmed at three that afternoon. Your driver's license had come in handy, too.

By then Amy and Benjy were ready, and we all piled into the car and drove to McDonald's. As we ate, we talked about other first days—the first day of kindergarten, the first day of junior high, and that scary first day in the big, new high school. You all interrupted each other with stories of embarrassing moments, awards, friendships, and frights.

After you had eaten, we hurried to buy notebook paper and compasses before I dropped you all at school—first Amy and Benjy at the middle school, then you.

"Bye, Mom," you said as you scooted across the seat, then stopped for a moment and looked back over your shoulder. "And, Mom . . . thanks."

It was the remnant of a kiss goodbye. It was the hesitancy of a little girl in ringlets beginning kindergarten. It was the anticipation of a young woman confident of her direction. All of it was in that gesture.

"I love you," was all I answered, but I hoped that somehow you could hear with your heart the rest of the words that were going through my mind. Words that told you how special you are to us. Words that would let you know how rich your father and I have been because you came into our lives. Words that tell you how much we believe in you, hope for you, pray for you, thank God for you.

As the school doors closed behind you and you disappeared into the corridor, I wanted so to holler after you . . . *WAIT! We have so much yet to do. We've never been to Hawaii. We've never taken a cruise. That book of poetry we wrote together isn't published yet. And what about the day we were going to spend at the cabin just being still and reading? Or the writers' workshop we planned to attend together in Illinois? You can't go yet . . . WAIT!*

But I knew that you couldn't wait—and that we could never keep you by calling a halt to your progress. You had promises to keep.

The things we want to save, Jesus said, must be let go, and the things we hold most tightly will be strangled in the end. And so, though I knew that this was a last first, I also knew somehow that it was a first in a lifetime of new beginnings . . . and I rejoiced!

September 3 — home

The children have been in school a week and a half, the summer vacation crafts bag has been unpacked and put away, and the bikes are being conditioned for winter. Memories of Mackinaw Island, fudge, convertible rides, and coconut suntan oil are leaking out between the clapboard siding of my mind and summer is leaking away, too, draining all its delicious nectar into the gray crack of winter.

Amy modeled at the State Fair and showed her horse at the 4-H Fair. With her horse she placed in every division—even got a first-place trophy in equitation. Now she's hankerin' for a new, "showier" horse.

Benjy's fishing tackle sits unnoticed in the corner, and Suzanne wonders where the time has gone for writing and thinking and dreaming. Bill's tan is fading, and the old convertible has been out only once this week. Yesterday a maple tree's leaves were turning red around the edges and the radio announcer was giving the football scores. I found the cider jugs and picked up sticks and pine cones . . . and kids from school. This morning I could see my breath.

September 8 — home

Bill and I went to Indianapolis Monday night—dressed up for dinner and a movie, then checked into the Hyatt and gave each other our full attention. Then we ate breakfast together at The Porch, and he left for Nashville to take a Vocal Band picture. I'm

so glad that he thinks our love is important enough to go on
nurturing it and celebrating it. He's a rare man.

October 8 — home

The leaves are falling, and we've had a few days cool enough for
a fire in the fireplace. It is dangerously dry, so we're hoping
for rain before the ground freezes. The creek at the cabin is
completely dried up for the first time since we've been coming
here, and the pond is very, very low.

Perhaps it's the dryness, but for whatever reason the colors have
been outrageous this year. It isn't safe for me to be loose on the
highway, because the trees have my attention and that doesn't
leave enough for driving.

This afternoon, Bill and I went for a bike ride. We must have
ridden ten miles. What a perfect fall day! I think biking is a
romantic thing to do, and a great time to talk.

Life is good. We are so blessed!

October 11 — home

The kids have had breakfast and gone to school. Bill's at the
office. I've mopped the floor, washed the sheets, washed dishes,
and straightened things. The fire is burning low, and all is still. I
take this moment in gratitude like the small morsel of bread at
communion—hold it, consider its meaning, make it a part of me,
knowing the cost of it.

A prayer for the children, now in the influence of their peers,
for strength and integrity, and that all will go well while we are
gone on tour, and that loneliness will not color their value
judgments and decision making.

A prayer for Bill, that he will be able to stand tall under the tremendous load of responsibility he carries daily—that his brain won't splinter from all the details that crowd him, that I will love him so well that he will be always operating from a secure home base in an insecure and confused society.

A prayer for the concerts and the people who are planning now to attend, for their hurts and brokenness, for their need to celebrate and experience joy, for the unity of true believers and their realization that Your kingdom has indeed come—and shall one day be visible even to the blind.

A prayer for me, that I will be swift at putting aside my fears and awareness of my inadequacies and not waste too much precious energy on turning my attention to myself, that I will quickly and with grace submit my whole self to be used with no consciousness of saving my own ego. May I truly "treat triumph and disaster just the same." May I center on His power for all my needs.

A prayer for Mother and Melody, who stay with the children when we must be gone—that they will not be too tired to enjoy each other, and that the children will be unselfish and considerate.

A prayer for all the staff at home and the crew on the road who do those thankless jobs that make or break a trip. May they feel loved and valued.

And for the group—for Gary and the singers, for the brass and the rhythm players, that they won't get so tired of hearing the same lines and songs that they lose their enthusiasm and focus. May my singing not grate on their nerves unbearably.

This moment is filled to the brim. The day is calling.

October 18 — fall tour, on the road

I so hated to leave the kids this time. What a gift they are—so willing, so caring about what we're doing, so responsible. We could never function as we do if it weren't for their commitment and Mother, Annie, Lela, Melody,* and all the people who help.

We had worship together by the kitchen fire last night. Suzanne read from Isaiah for our encouragement, and Amy read "No Man Is an Island." We talked about how each of us functions as a part of the whole, and that when anyone is hurt or dies or is in trouble, we are all damaged by it a little. Being loved is the greatest thing!

October 19 — Toronto

Toronto—so new and clean and hopeful. Still flourishing, still building. It will be interesting to see at what point the apex is reached, when graft and greed start sucking the life away, when growth stops and decline begins, when the earth's best efforts are pulled to the earth and returned to dust.

---

*Annie is Bill's aunt, who helped me hold my household together. Melody is my niece, my sister's oldest daughter, who helped with the children.

October 21 – Buffalo, New York

Windy. Cold.

October 30 – Charleston, South Carolina

It's been more than a week since I wrote. The concerts have gone well, but the crowds have been a little down in some places. We went from Buffalo to Maine. What a beautiful drive through New England (around Boston)! The trees were beautiful, banked up around the layered hillsides. In Portland, Carol McSpadden and I shopped a little for the kids and others back home.

After Portland, we went to Philly, where half the audience was Italian and *loved* Carman. We drove on to Akron because we had Sunday off. We stayed at the Quaker Square and had a much-needed rest. We had a good leisurely meal, and Bill and I enjoyed each other and the quiet.

Going to a movie, we met a taxi driver whose wife had sued him for divorce because he wasn't making enough to make ends meet. They had a two-month-old baby. He seemed so broken and shook up. Bill invited him to the concert, but we didn't see him if he came. At our devotion time with the group, we prayed for him and his family, that somehow the Holy Spirit would draw them to Himself.

After Akron came Columbus, then we went home for a day on our way to Nashville. Our house was all torn up with remodeling, but it was good to be home, just the same. The kids were out of school because of teachers' institute, so they went on with us to Nashville. They were so excited to go that they could hardly eat or pack. The kids always look forward to being with their Nashville friends.

We drove all night to Greensboro, where we had an energetic and warm concert. There were fifty-three Gaithers there—the

North Carolina branch. They all got together and came in a group. Bill's cousin, Anita, and her husband, Dick, flew out from home to be with them.

Tonight we're ending up in Charleston, and I am sure 'nough ready to go home. We leave again Wednesday night for Praise Gathering.

November 10 — home

Tour is over, Praise Gathering is history, and Benjy's sick with infected tonsils. He woke up in the Hyatt Sunday morning with a high fever and a sore throat and has barely been able to lift his head from the pillow until today. The fever has finally broken, so we've been reading some books and doing homework.

Praise Gathering was unique and wonderful. Each year there is a new milestone, something new to learn, something new to decide.

We all came home exhausted, but full and empowered.

Today I have to speak in Muncie and have had a struggle deciding what to speak about. I have learned, though, to do what I know to do and leave the rest with the Lord. . . .

(Later . . .) I can't believe how the Spirit always makes up the difference between what we have to give and what the people need. The talk I gave was so simple, so ordinary, yet somehow it was just right. I was so tired, but there was a peace about what I needed to say, and when the time came it seemed to flow easily. There were tears of release and discovery. There were people who came up afterward to share the stories of their points of need that had been touched. Amazing . . . and from so little!

December 26 — the cabin

Even blindfolded I would recognize the specialness of this moment, and I see it with such focus that I almost have to turn my eyes away.

I want to cry out like Thornton Wilder's Emily, "Oh, wait. Look at me. It goes so fast and we don't have time to look at one another." Only we *are* looking at one another, and I have a feeling that, deep inside, all of us—even the children—know that things are moving by us. But tonight we are here, and we love each other.

Benjy has his friend Glenn here, and they are playing Scrabble and the Nerf Ping-Pong that Benjy got for Christmas. Amy and Suzanne are singing and playing the piano, playing dominoes and Sorry. Bill and Suzanne's boyfriend are deep in a game of checkers. Everyone is talking, laughing, singing, or thinking.

Suzanne seems more serious since her eighteenth birthday, needs more hugs, and wants to do things "we've always done" with even greater attention to the details of traditions that have grown as she has.

We had a beautiful Christmas with lots of secrets and time for savoring each gift and celebrating what we mean to each other. Suzanne got me a beautiful knitted mohair coat with a separate cape. She spent much too much of her hard-earned money. But her sacrifice was precious to me, and even more precious was the note that came with it.

Benjy gave me some gloves and five dollars that he thought I could spend on myself. Amy got me a hearth broom, some Gloria Vanderbilt perfume, and some wicker.

Bill got me New York—that is, we decided to give a trip there to each other. We saw some plays and the glorious "Christmas Spectacular" at Radio City Music Hall; it was truly spectacular. Our dear friends, Dan and Sue Johnson, met us there, and we grew to love them even more during that packed-full three days.

1982

The snow fell silently the last day and covered the city. Little white lights glittered everywhere from clumps of fir trees along the streets. The skaters glided along the ice in Rockefeller Center under the gaze of the three-story-high angels and the huge New York Christmas tree. We ate at the top of the RCA building (sixty-seventh floor) in the Rainbow Room and watched the temperature drop on the huge thermometer on the skyscraper just outside the window.

Bill was a wonderful adventurer and a skillful lover. We built memories to draw from for the rest of our lives. Memories are perhaps the best gifts of all.

The Trio did a concert at the Anderson Gym on December 6 for the people of our county who have been out of work. The proceeds will help with fuel bills and food for the winter. It was a whole community effort and a great happening. We ended up with eight thousand people and made about thirty thousand dollars for them. There was a tremendous feeling of brotherhood and caring in a town so hard hit by economic depression. Somehow, though, hard times give people the chance to reveal their true character, to share with those even less fortunate, to encourage and to look up together.

Then, for Suzanne's birthday, we went to Farrell's. We hadn't done that since the year Daddy died. That party had turned out to be so painful—our efforts to be cheerful and happy—that we didn't try it again for these eight years. But this year we went with Lisa* and Suzanne's friend (and our family) and it was fun. Afterward we shopped a little and looked in windows. Everything was all aglitter for Christmas, and people seemed friendly.

Doesn't seem that she could be eighteen. What a joy she has been!

*My sister Evelyn's youngest daughter.

1983

We deal with reality at two points in our lives —
birth and death. If only we could always live our days
with as clear a vision of the things that matter
as we do at those two times.

January 3 — home

Back at work—this time on a new Christmas musical
to communicate the message of "He Started the Whole
World Singing."

I've been toying with the idea of "glory," in the sense of that
something more that makes life have some eternal value, even here.
It is what life had in the very beginning. It is what was lost with
humanity's loss of innocence. And it is what was returned to us in
Jesus the Messiah. Today I wrote a lyric about this called "Bring
Back the Glory."

A couple of days after Christmas, Bill's Dad had some sort of
heart attack. At first he thought it was a cold and indigestion,
but by evening he had chest pains. Lela took him to the hospital,
and they admitted him. There does not seem to have been
extensive damage, but George does definitely feel it was his heart.

The children are quite concerned. I think they are so aware of
the seriousness because of their experience when Daddy died.
Amy has been very philosophical about it and about the end of
the world—her future and life and death in general. Benjy
wanted to know what Grandpa looks like; he hasn't been able to
see him since he's been in intensive care. Suzanne just discusses
it openly—the effect death would have on Grandma if Grandpa
died and vice versa.

January 7 — home

I've been writing this week—songs and the Christmas musical.
Bill George came up from Nashville, and wrote music for some
lyrics and ideas I had.

It's been both a good and bad week. I always dread the pressures of returning to the job—not the writing, but to the kids going back to school and Bill back to the office. Everyone becomes so edgy, the kids argue, Bill's more short-tempered, and I feel like exploding with the pressure of keeping things on any kind of even keel. That makes me more uptight.

January 10 — the cabin

I think this musical will be special, and I'm excited about the message. The pieces just seem to keep falling into place.

I'm always amazed at the way the Lord gives us just what we need when we need it. I found an old tape in the cupboards; it was labeled "Bill—new song." I don't know how long it had been around, but just out of curiosity, I listened to it. It perfectly fit a song idea I needed, "Jesus—What A Lovely Name." I wrote that lyric and finished the song.

Today, I was needing a piece of music to fit the spirit of Simeon's announcement as well as the verse from John 1, a lyric about "We have seen his glory."* There was a melody Bill George and Bill had written a few weeks ago simply labeled "Christmas Carol," and it will work perfectly. So I work on.

Benjy gets a new pair of glasses today. He can't see the board at school.

January 20 — home

George is at St. Vincent's Hospital. He had his catheterization, which showed two totally blocked arteries and two 80 percent and 90 percent blocked.

Bill went to stay with Lela the night before last and then went

*John 1:14, paraphrased.

back this morning to either bring George home for a three-week wait for his turn at surgery or to see if he can have the surgery moved up. George had another attack last Friday, so was already at Community again before the catheterization. His condition seems quite serious and must be dealt with.

Lela looked so small and brave in that little motel room last night. She has not left his side since all of this began. There has come the time in Bill's life to switch roles with the two people who have always "been there" for him, who have been consistent and strong and accountable. Now the "child is father of the man," and must let them lean on him. It has meant so much to Lela to have Bill "be there."

Yes, we deal with reality at two points in our lives—birth and death. If only we could always live our days with as clear a vision of the things that matter as we do at those two times.

February 3 — home

Last week was like no other we've ever lived through. Monday we got word that George would have his surgery on Tuesday. Bill went down and stayed Monday night with Lela, then stayed all through the waiting time—not knowing, just waiting. I had to speak at a retreat in Iowa on Tuesday, so had to leave Monday night.

All day Tuesday at the retreat, I waited for word about George, and when I had a break in my speaking schedule, I kept calling back. The surgery went smoothly and everything was good.

I flew home after the retreat and went straight to the hospital. George was doing well, but I felt Bill and I should stay because no one else was there with Lela by then. We checked in at the Martin House for the night and then had breakfast with Lela the next morning. We took turns seeing George for the ten minutes allowed us every two hours.

George is having some trouble getting his pulse rate stabilized. How I pray for George and Lela both, that they will feel God near them. How I pray for wisdom and courage to know what and when—and how!—to speak and help.

February 10 — home

New day. A Thursday. Bill's been in Nashville since Tuesday working on the Vocal Band album. George came home yesterday and is seemingly doing all right. He has had quite a struggle with his pulse rate. I know not being strong for a while will be hard for him.

My heart feels troubled today—so much I need to know and have resolved: projects to finish, relationships I need time to nurture.

Benjy is suddenly washing his hair every morning and has been wearing his glasses. He wanted me to take him shopping for shirts the other day. I wonder why all this new attention to physical appearance.

March 3 — home

Tomorrow I will be forty-one. Strange, I don't feel older, except for the difficulty I have keeping my hips from expanding and the fact that when I look down at a mirror lying on a table, I see my face sagging like the jaws of a bulldog. So, I'm exercising more and trying to look up to keep my face in place.

But this morning when I got up, I still felt the same excitement over the gift of a new day, and when I walked out into the predawn darkness I could still smell the earth thawing from winter.

Yesterday as I was driving to town with Suzanne, my stomach was quivery with excitement, and I didn't know why, except that I love being alive and it's almost spring. After supper, when Bill and I walked the mile or so to his folks' house, I felt like skipping, and the sunset made me catch my breath.

And I still have that "I-wonder-what-I'll-be-when-I-grow-up" feeling, like my life is just beginning. There is so much I'd like to do and be and learn; the things I've done already seem like interesting classes I've taken to prepare for something yet to come.

There's a hunger in me to travel and experience things, not as a part of our work, but just to absorb life. I want to do that with Bill and the children while we have each other. I'd like to ride to the bottom of the Grand Canyon on horseback and spend the night in a cave. I want to make love in the warm sand on the seashore. I want to join an archaeological expedition in the land of the Bible. I want to watch our children's faces as they discover physical exhaustion and the bliss of rest. I want to have to depend on each other for survival and entertainment so that we have stories to share and secrets known only to us.

We're getting to the place in our lives where actually being able to do these things is in our reach, but the stamina may be slipping away. And our time together as a family is at a premium—this is our last year to have Suzanne in the house full time. And just when we've learned how to notice and what to look for, our chances to pass that on to little ones are almost gone. There must be an eternity!

So, "she's just passed 40," they say, as if that means I've arrived or, in some cases, gone past counting. But I know inside I'm the same sometimes confident, sometimes insecure kid I was in

Burlington, Michigan, playing Blind Man's Bluff and wondering what I'll turn out to be.

March 18 — spring tour, Pittsburgh

It was so hard to leave this morning. The kids wanted so to come; their hearts are here. But their heads have to stay in school, though I doubt they did very well concentrating today. I woke them at six—bigger, more mature bodies now snuggled warm in their beds, but still children, still trusting, still so vulnerable. Suzanne tucked a note into Bill's case to be read later:

> Dear Mom and Dad:
> I just wanted to write you a little note to tell you how much I love you. I think we'll do OK this time, and I don't want you to worry about us. Just think about the people in the concerts and what you are going to say to them. Even though it may be an inconvenience for you to go sometimes, I feel that it is what God wants you to do, and I'm proud of your decision to speak to the people. Just remember when you're on the road, your three biggest supporters and fans will be behind you here at home. I love you!
>
> Suzanne

The responsibility demanded of those three is great, but the way they keep rising to the demands on them is so special to us. We're glad they feel a part of what we are trying to do—that is the most important thing of all.

March 19 — Lakeland, Florida

We almost fell over this evening when we walked into the arena to find George and Lela standing in the hallway. They had driven down to surprise us, and they certainly did!

George seemed to be feeling great, and Lela said he'd planned this little coup ever since he was in the hospital. It was good to see them and to know they are having such a good time together. They'd gotten an apartment since there were no motels available. Some lady who ran a motel had a friend who'd made an apartment for her son, and she rented it to them.

The concert tonight was one of the best ever. The audience was so ready, and the energy was high.

March 22 — Shreveport

New day. Bright, cool, and crisp—too crisp to lie in the sun, so I think I'll go to a mall while Bill and the guys play tennis. I'm really missing the kids today and excited to have Suzanne come to Chattanooga.

(Later. . . .)Went to the mall and got things for the kids' Easter baskets. They still love to get baskets, even though they're really too big. As long as they love them, I love to fix them.

April 27 — Portland, Oregon

We've come from the concert last night in California, up through Oregon on our way to Spokane—a long trip that will barely get us in, even driving straight through. We watched the sun come bursting over the fog-veiled foothills this morning, while the smoke of wood fires curled its way skyward from the chimneys of tiny farm houses. Tall, black pines pointed their fingers to the heavens, and the yellow bushes, wild plum, and crab apple are all in glorious bloom, splashing their vibrant color against a ground of green. Lewis and Clark must have known God to have had Him breathing down their necks like this.

Last night was a new place, and the concert seemed laid-back. We met together in an upper room and had communion. Carman's mother had baked some loaves of Italian bread, and I got some grape juice, so the table was spread. One of the band members led devotions, Bill led several songs of commitment and devotion, two other band members prayed. It was a warm, loving time.

We're driving through Portland with Mt. Hood in front of us and Mt. St. Helens to our left. Mt. St. Helens has a new shape since the eruption and looks flat on top. They say that a cubic mile of it was blown away and sprinkled all over this valley.

Suzanne and Benjy will be out tomorrow night in Seattle. I'm so eager to see them and squeeze their strong little bodies.

May 1 — Wyoming

9:15 P.M. Long drive since last night in Portland—all day and all last night, and still we have far to go. We've spent this day talking, playing dictionary, eating junk food, and sharing tapes.

Suzanne and Benjy came out to Seattle. They had to bring several boxes of songbooks and Trio tapes, and they ran into an accident on the way to the airport, so they missed their plane and Suzanne had to find another flight. They got in around 9:30, and we were glad to see them! It has been so good to have them along.

In Seattle, Bill and I went out to lie in the sun. It wasn't very hot, but it was beautiful with the mountains towering in the background and the rhododendrons in bloom. The pines and the lilacs made everything smell like Eden.

May 7 — back home, at the cabin

Dear Suzanne:

I got up at 5:30 this morning and came out here to the cabin. I wanted to get alone long enough to think about what I should say tomorrow at the high school breakfast for graduating seniors. I'm not sure who will be there, but I want it to be special for your sake.

I can't believe you are graduating already, yet you are certainly more than ready. It seems only moments since Dad and I first brought you home to our little rented house next door to Grandma's and Grandpa's place. How excited and proud we were of our tiny black-haired miracle—so awake and alert, so bright and sensitive. I remember how your little face would strain to understand, almost come to a point, as you concentrated and absorbed this new world you'd found yourself in. And your newness made everything new for us. As you discovered lights and textures, colors and sounds, it was for us like realizing them for the first time as well.

How discouraged I felt as a new mother! Your intensity made you such a complicated child. You cried easily when you got too much excitement, which caused fatigue and colic. Sometimes you'd cry so long that I'd end up in tears, too, and have to call for help. Lela would always come over from next door to calm you, or Bill would hold you close to his warm skin and you would sleep at last.

Such a joy you've been. It's a good thing children don't really comprehend how very loved they are; it would be a burden to them. Yet as much as is possible, you've been a child who realized love and was so responsive to it. Since the first day you reached your little hand to touch my cheek—your first act of giving love to someone else—you've been finding ways of reaching out: to Daddy and me, to your grandparents, to dear Aunt Lillie, to children, to old people, and to those in need.

And now you wear a cap and gown. As the tassel shifts, so do all of our lives, to make way for a solo stanza in the song of your existence. Yet we always sing the choruses together—around campfires, on beaches, in tour busses, at bedtime, in summer, at the breakfast table, after late night dates. And the song is "joy."

June 26 — Hyannis Port, Massachusetts

We are finally here waiting to board the 9:00 A.M. ferry to Nantucket. Beautiful morning—sunny, but slightly overcast.

With five families of us packed into the bus like sardines in a can of mustard sauce, we laughed, talked, slept, and ate our way to Massachusetts, stopping once in a little Pennsylvania town to have a pizza picnic.

We feel like natives here, and part of our "homeless" stays here when we leave. It is by now a very familiar place for the children. They have memories piled high on every cobblestone street and familiar beach. This year they are feeling very independent and want to make it around on their own. Benjy has discovered girls, and instead of not wanting to be around them, he is enjoying being outnumbered.

This summer and this trip are filled with where we are. Bill and I are feeling a little more freedom to talk a little longer or walk with the other couples, knowing the kids are responsible and having a happy time. We are able to play group games with everyone taking part now, because the children are "old enough." We are no longer needed so much for physical care and protection or to entertain and instruct. But we are needed more than ever for emotional and spiritual support and inspiration.

June 29 — Nantucket

Amy and I are at the Morning Glory Cafe on the South Wharf.
This morning we needed some time alone, so we came here early.
We've been talking and watching the fishermen and shopkeepers
starting their days. Everything is all crisp and fresh from the rain,
and the sea, pretending it didn't throw a tantrum yesterday, is
lying quietly like a spent child at rest.

On the news last night we learned that a bridge we came across
the day before yesterday in our bus loaded with families had
collapsed, sending two trucks and a car to the river seventy-five
feet below. Three people were killed, others injured. We will take
another route home, thankful to be alive.

Amy and I have had our coffee and English tea—and a good
conversation. I also had one of those marvelous Morning Glory
muffins while she nibbled at blueberry pancakes. By now the
others are stirring back at the cottage, and we promised to meet
Bill at the French restaurant. It will be our second breakfast, but
we'll never tell!

June 30 — Nantucket

Time is passing so swiftly. This place has woven us into its fabric once more. Yet there are threads that will stay a part of the pattern of what we are: sun-bleached threads, sea-green threads, fine, misty gray threads, sea-gull-white threads. Today at surfside the children, big and little, are building sand castles and riding waves.

There are no clouds in the skies—only an occasional sea gull gliding low to scavenge bits of basket lunches. A yellow, red, and blue striped kite with a very long, graceful tail is hovering over the dunes, and a white jet trail diagonally crosses the uninterrupted blue.

I notice, a little sadly, a relaxing of rules about keeping this island simple and quaint. Greed for the mighty dollar is eventually earth's undoing. It is the omnivorous monster that in time devours its own children.

The desire to squeeze in more tourists will result in the tourists' destroying what they came here to experience! One day they will leave the place wasted, then move on to the next place of atmosphere and solitude to gobble it up as well. I am reminded of a giant game of Pac Man, with the islands the tiny dots devoured by the gaping mouths.

For us, this is a place of endings—of projects, of dreams, of childhoods, of innocence—but it is a place, too, of beginnings— of new ideas, new ventures, new dreams, and widened visions; of self-discovery and new chapters of growth.

For Benjy, this year's trip to the island celebrates the beginning of his awareness of himself and the importance of relationships. For Suzanne, it marks the end of childhood and the beginning of adulthood's commitments and responsibilities. For Amy, this place sees the birth of her confidence in what she is becoming and gives expression to the joy in what she is. She likes herself this year, revels in the love of family and friends, and appreciates her unique talents and opportunities.

1 9 8 3

For me, this space in time is a kaleidoscope of beginnings and endings, a crazy quilt of mixed emotions. Yet, somehow, the continuum of our coming to this island gives a consistency to it all. I am at peace with change, and I find tranquility in the knowing that "there's always a place to begin."

July 3 — Nantucket

Our last day here. I write as the others finish getting ready to walk to church—the ancient Congregational church at the top of the hill, the one with the tall steeple and stately bells. There we will worship as families have done for a century.

Bill and I got up early this morning to go to the Morning Glory on the wharf one last time. Hand in hand, we walked around the docks until the cafe opened, looking at the great yachts that had come in during the night.

It's always hard to say goodbye to this island. I know it may be childish, but I'd like to have a place here, just to make sure of our coming back, a sort of toehold of residency, a place of belonging.

Someday I will come here without a crowd and have time for luscious loneliness. But I'd like to have someone to talk to and love, someone who shares my need for solitude and my love for this salt-laden place.

For now, we have our last Morning Glory muffin-and-fruit breakfast and make ready to board the ferry. It's a clear, hot day. The sun is kind, and this gray land will soon become a beckoning dot on the horizon, fading once more into the warm mists of memory.

July 21 — home

Benjy is a teenager, and we celebrated this new era with a birthday party and band concert—his band. He was so nervous and excited about playing for the parents and friends that he hardly noticed his party. He couldn't eat and kept worrying about the details.

The weather threatened rain, and there were thunderstorms off and on all day long. Finally, the clouds cleared around four in the afternoon, and the boys set up their equipment on the back parking lot of the guest house.

After the wiener roast with sweet corn, baked beans, salad, and fresh fruit, we all went up and sat on the grass on the hillside. Benjy had designed a program cover with a graphic of their group's name, TRUTH*; I had typed out the list of songs and the personnel of the group; and Suzanne had duplicated the programs at the office for him. The band passed them out to the "audience," and the show got under way.

It was all rock music, of course, and not a totally preferred style to many adults, yet we all gave them enthusiastic applause and rapt attention.

After the numbers were finished, Benj and the whole group filed rather dejectedly into the guest house. Bill leaped to his feet and ran after them. When he found them inside, they were sitting around rather discouraged, recounting all the mistakes they'd made and wondering if they'd failed. Bill began to tell them how well they'd done, how hard they'd worked, and how proud he was of their discipline. Benjy brightened up.

"Really?" he asked. "You mean it? You think it was okay?" Then the boys began to talk excitedly among themselves and to Bill, reviewing all the good moments in the concert, analyzing the hard places, and remembering the times they'd forgotten the words.

Bill told them they needed to go outside to talk to their audience. Out they burst with their excitement growing with each hug, handshake, and compliment.

After the dads helped the band tear down all the equipment, load it all onto Grandpa's truck, and then carry it back down to the basement, they all came back to the gazebo so Benjy could cut

*His group has since become VYNTURE and is still playing and writing songs together.

his cake and hear us sing "Happy Birthday!" They were all back in the real world again, but a little more grown up and a little more sure of their place and worth.

After the party was over and everyone was gone, Benjy called me to his room to tuck him in. He was still basking in his daddy's approval. "Did you see Dad? He led a standing ovation!"

We prayed together, thanking God for sending us this special little boy, and for allowing us to be a family. I doctored his foot and elbow (he'd had a bad fall trying to jump onto the diving board earlier that afternoon), and he figured out how to lie so that the knot on his bruised head wouldn't touch the pillow. Then he fell quickly off to sleep, a boy again, exhausted and happy.

July 25 — home

Amy is soaring. Two very successful performances of *The Sound of Music* are behind her, and there were strong reviews of her first major role (Liesel). The theater last night was full and the applause enthusiastic. The hallway backstage after the performance was filled with people waiting to congratulate Amy for her performance, and she loved every minute of it.

And she said so: "I could love doing this, Mother! Yes ! I love it!" She loves the work, the planning, the rehearsals, the waiting, the singing, the dancing, and the acting. She loves opening nights and curtain calls ("That may be my favorite part of all!"), costuming and makeup, blocking scenes and choreography. And she's good—as fluid and natural as a mountain spring, as sparkling and energetic as noontime sunbeams on a waterfall.

Bill and I got her a dozen yellow roses. Bill signed the card and laid them in her room while she was sleeping yesterday afternoon. Suzanne took pictures. Benjy told her she did a good job and gave her a big hug.

Friday night I went with her and the cast and their parents to Pizza Hut. She floated like a butterfly from table to table talking with each new friend she'd made—and she has made friends easily.

Today will be the final performance and a party. We're letting her go to this performance and party alone. There are several children in the cast who will be there, so we feel it will be all right for her to go without us.

How do I feel about the kids and their talent? Proud and scared. Talent will not be ignored and can take them in many directions. The direction depends upon their choices. I'm praying more and trusting more as I feel our control giving way to their self-control.

Next week Suzanne and I will go to look at her dorm room and buy things for it. A new chapter for her, too. And for me, more letting go and more praying.

August 7 — home

I went with Joanne this week and registered for a class at Ball State on Emerson and Thoreau. I'm very excited about it. I hope someday I can finish my Master's and even my Doctorate. I may be dreaming, but I'd like to teach in college after the kids get out of high school. Maybe I don't even remember how to teach, but I feel as though I've been teaching all along.

I am so tired. I don't think you can be alive and be this tired. We've had company for two weeks straight. I enjoy people, but I am so weary.

I am still waiting and praying about tour. Something needs to work out with the children, and I don't know what. I do know Mother can't go on as she has in the past because of her health. I will pray for a sign as to whether I should stop traveling or go on. If I go on, I need to know that emotional and spiritual stability will be maintained at home.

The ideal situation could be that my sister, Evelyn, could live here and be available to step into our household when we have to be gone. But that seems impossible. Her husband, Dave, is an engineer; the likelihood of his getting a new position in our depressed area of automotive plants is very slim.

September 20 – home

I'm lonely today. Lonely for Suzanne, lonely for Daddy, lonely for my childhood and for our children's childhoods. Sometimes it seems that the lives we work so hard to build turn on us and become our master; the fortifications we construct to protect the things we love and believe in become prisons that hold us instead.

I feel restless and would walk away from all we have built and start anew, vulnerable and excited . . . yet not afraid. I feel like a cicada whose skin has become a shell, dry and stiff. I feel that shell splitting the middle, and though I know it will mean exposing new skin to the sun, I am curious about what lies out there and eager to break out. If we wait too long, the shell may become a tomb.

September 28 – (Wednesday before Praise Gathering) Indianapolis Hyatt

How to begin? So much spinning in my head . . .

Last night was my last class in Emerson before a midterm coming up Tuesday after we get home from here . . . rehearsals after class and again this morning . . . moving the whole family into the hotel, parking, and remembering details—for us, for my workshop, for the kids.

A piece Bill wants me to write about Ethel Waters for Thursday night . . . final notes to make for the workshop . . . books I need that didn't come . . . displays to set up. An introduction that Bill expects to be "stunning" (whatever that is!) to "Then Came the Morning" for Saturday night's concert . . . new material to memorize for the trio concert . . . two morning prayer meetings for which I need to prepare devotional thoughts.

Such a need inside my heart for quiet, for peace, for thought . . . body aching from a cold . . . a scheduled meeting with the Secretary of State and other Christian leaders . . . trying to remember people's names and faces.

Lord, quiet my heart. Give me the thoughts and plans you want me to have so I can give them to those who will come. Let me not be impatient with myself, with Bill, or with the children in my eagerness to be efficient and alert. Help me to worry about only one thing at a time—the thing I can just now affect.

October 7 – Saginaw, Michigan (fall tour)

It's green here—such a contrast to the dry, brown landscape we left at home. It's been the driest summer since 1936, the newscasters tell us, yet the trees are turning color and the apples are on.

The concert went pretty well last night, except that I *felt* nothing. There are so many reasons. I hope God gives me a little ray of insight and revelation. I know He's there, and I don't doubt that. I can go without feeling, but it sure is hard when I don't sing well and then can't feel either. Maybe tonight will live for me.

October 8 — Lansing, Michigan

Good night last night. Saginaw did come alive—almost Fully Alive.

October 12 — The Cedars, Washington, D.C.*

Quiet, blessed quiet! I do so need to be still.

This place is an oasis in this town and in our schedule, a place where we are surrounded by the fragrance of servanthood, as these lovely people minister so royally to us who are so unworthy. I want to be a better servant, so that I can touch someone with the healing balm that has so lovingly been given to us here.

It has been a hard week. I have been hurtful because of my poor judgment—again. Because I questioned Bill's wisdom in dealing with Amy this weekend, I left him discouraged and alienated to the point of wanting to withdraw from the whole parenting role.

I don't know how to deal with all this. I feel we need to be free to disagree, but I have to learn to keep my mouth shut more, to trust his judgment more and not always have to be the deciding voice. I keep acting as if I'm judge and jury of what is right and fair.

*The Cedars is an elegant old house and grounds that have been preserved and dedicated to ministering to statesmen, world leaders, and sojourning Christians who are in need of restoration and community.

Today I will work on my Thoreau paper and try to listen to the Lord's word for me. He is always so faithful; I am most often so foolish.

November 17 — home

So many things have happened since I wrote; there's no place to begin. Vocal Band had a week tour in September and are now gone again for a long weekend. I just finished my class in Emerson, Thoreau, and Whitman and loved every minute of it. But it has been hard to juggle everything at times, especially since Annie fell and hurt her hip and I've had all the housework to do, too. I'm so behind!

The most exciting thing is that Dave got a job at Delco and Dave and Evelyn will be moving here soon. I believe that is a real answer to prayer. I asked the Lord to give me a sign if He wanted me to keep traveling. I believe He has. It will be so good to have Evelyn close, too.

November 30 — home

Had he lived, yesterday would have been Daddy's seventy-sixth birthday. Sometimes I still miss him like he's still here, only gone somewhere, and I find myself waiting for a chance to go home or for him to come home. When things are confused and complicated for me, I think of him as though having home the same would make everything else in the world normal again.

I'm almost ready for Christmas—most of the gifts are wrapped, and the tree is up. Bill and I had intended to go to New York tomorrow, just the two of us, but we decided there wasn't time if we kept anything going here at home with all the other activities and obligations we have committed to do. I was disappointed, but I'm sure there will be another time—maybe after Christmas.

I start a new class tonight. I hope I don't have to drop it because I find it's more than I can handle. I love learning and studying again. There is something in me that would like to stop doing all else and become a full-time student so my energies wouldn't be so divided.

Suzanne just came home to practice her piano. Benjy went to do a recording session, and Amy is at her flute lesson and flute choir rehearsal. My body urges me to rest; sleep will clear away the cobwebs and make me new tomorrow.

December 8 — Pittsburgh

I suppose all that can be said comparing clouds to doubt has been said, but there is a new awareness of it for me.

We just flew through blue, clear skies from Norfolk all the way to Pittsburgh. The sun was warm, and we could see for miles. Only when we began our descent into the Pittsburgh area did we become aware of a thick, billowy floor of cloud cover beneath us.

The clouds were beautiful, all edged in the pink of late afternoon, fluffy and soft, unthreatening as we looked down on them from above, where the sun still reigned in all its obvious and tangible glory.

But we had to descend, and as the plane plunged through those fluffy-looking clouds we began to lose our sight. Everything turned gray, and all visibility disappeared. I found myself hoping that the pilot—and other pilots—were paying close attention to the signals from the control tower and to communications from each other.

It seemed like a long time before we could see where we were going. By that time the landing gear was down, the announcement had been made to fasten seat belts and return chair-backs to "their upright and locked positions," and the plane had made its irrevocable move to align itself to what the pilot trusted to be the position of the runway.

We are now on the ground. It is dark here. Oh, darkness
was a fact of this day all along. but here on the ground darkness
came prematurely. Up there, up above the clouds, it is still late
afternoon, bathed in the soft pink glow of a warm and benevolent
sun. The cover that had been so lovely when it was a floor
beneath us and we soared above it in glorious sight is now
our ceiling. It hovers, low and foreboding, shutting away the
rays that would warm us and give us light.

What is it about us human beings that makes us believe that
the way things seem at the moment is how they really are? How
soon we adjust to and accept blindness or sight, warmth or chill,
darkness or light, and think it shall ever be so.

It is sight that should sustain us through the clouds, making us
believers in life, "cockeyed optimists" in a pessimistic culture,
because we know about and have embraced the Light. And when
the sun is shining, why do we not store up its light in the dark
places of our souls and memorize its beauty, charging our energies
with its power so that we can draw from its collected reality when
the seeing has faded for a time.

Last Sunday at church, two weeks into Advent, a young girl lit
two candles to commemorate our Christmas celebration: the
prophet's candle and the Bethlehem candle. It was the Bethlehem
candle that was new that week, and the scripture the girl read
following the lighting was about Bethlehem and the coming of the
Christ child to that insignificant place.

As the girl read, the new candle burned stronger and brighter, as
if with the reality of the Messiah's coming to our space/time earth.
As she read the sacred works, however, the prophet's candle began
to slowly fade, until by the time the child was announced, the flame
of prophecy had extinguished itself completely.

Perhaps it was a sense of fulfillment that made it sleep, secure
in the knowledge that its job had been done. Perhaps it was the
quiet knowing that voices and torches of faith are not needed
when reality burns its way through the darkness.

For whatever reason, Prophecy disappeared. But the reality of
God-with-us burned brightly to inspire our worship.

Here on the ground in the dark and cold, we need the candle

and the flame . . . they make us remember and not grow weary in hope or tired of confirming a fact hidden deep in our hearts.

December 24 ~ home, early morning

The kids and Bill are still asleep, bedded down in our bedroom before the fire. The night was alarmingly cold, way below zero, and there was a bit of new snow. All the fireplaces in the house are burning, and both the furnaces came on because of the wind.

Last night we all snuggled into our room between piles of blankets while I finished reading *The Greatest Christmas Pageant Ever.* Then, while all the candles and the fire burned, we talked and listened to tapes until we fell asleep.

Today is Christmas Eve. Once again we search for places to house the Christ and seek to enlarge the place we have already offered Him.

(Later . . .) I'm cooking a ham and perking some wassail for our celebration tonight. Bill and Benjy just filled the wood box and went to Mother's to thaw out the swans, which are trapped by frozen ice in the creek. The bitter cold is dangerous and could be fatal if one were to be caught out in it for long.

Fifteen below. Yet this house is a warm cocoon, and we wrap it around ourselves by some primitive instinct to fortify ourselves against the raging elements outside.

December 29 — New York City

What a ploy! We did squeeze out time and money to come to New York with the whole family for three whole days.

We've had a wonderful time walking the wet streets still decorated with thousands of white Christmas lights. Evergreen boughs everywhere—white enameled twigs and red bows. Riding in a horse-drawn, covered carriage through Central Park in the rain. Having breakfast of fruit and croissants at the Plaza.

Waiting with the noisy ethnic crowds at Mama Leone's for a table in the ancient room filled with fifteen-foot paintings, Italian sculpture and a huge old Christmas tree. Poor Suzanne about fainted from hunger before we finally were seated and was almost past eating. But we ordered pasta and salad and had a great time talking and speculating about the young couple who happened to be seated at a table for two right beside the grand derriere of a nude statue. (Was it their first date? How embarrassing!)

Just now I have stolen out of the room while everyone else is still asleep to sit in this typically New York cafe here in the hotel, have a muffin and some coffee, and watch the city coming to life. . . .

Amy is so taken with the whole idea of acting and the arts. She would love to perform here. She loves the city and all the excitement. How I pray that she will find a place for her talents in God's total scheme. What energy and drive! What an immense potential for good . . . or for failure if frustrated and wasted.

Suzanne is fighting feeling insignificant right now. She is so involved in filling requirements and making grades that it's hard to keep the whole in perspective. How I pray that she will not retreat into security . . . and obscurity. Risking takes so much courage and energy, and she seems so afraid sometimes . . . and weary.

Benjy. So much going on inside his little head, and it scares me that he doesn't let us have a glimpse of what he's thinking nearly often enough. And when he does, it's sometimes a surprising mixture of true facts and false conclusions. Other times he is so accurate in nailing reality to the wall that it almost takes my breath away.

Bill. Still growing, still changing, still inventing new ways and directions. Still pushing me, sometimes too hard until I feel used, sometimes until I feel encouraged and inspired.

Me. I feel like some caterpillar inside a cocoon, enjoying a moment of rest and security, yet stirred by some kind of disturbing certainty that change is coming and will call for a great deal of struggle—maybe pain, certainly work!

I must go wake the kids. We have tickets to the Radio City Music Hall's Christmas Spectacular.

1984

Big Brother has taken over half the earth, but I am still in charge of me!

January 5 — the cabin

The cold has broken, and so has a new year. 1984. And what is more, George Orwell was only partly right. Big Brother has taken over half the earth, but I am still in charge of me! And love still reigns where simple hearts surrender to its sovereignty and stand up to refuse the lords of earth.

Children still are running, singing in the streets, and somewhere music still is floating on the breeze at break of day. There are still some looking for and finding lovely ways to serve their brothers. Institutions still have yet to take the place of mother love and nurture. There are homes across the land, still nature's habitat for fledgling humankind. And folks still find there's joy and warmth in friendship and a smile.

The miles still wind their way across the amber waves of grain. And purple mountains, still majestic, lift our sights from the mundane and ordinary and call us to keep reaching for our dreams. There are streams somewhere from which it still is safe to drink the water, flowing crystal from the summit snow.

And while it's so that wars are rumored all throughout the world and flags unfurled are spat upon and burned in effigy, still peace and blessed tranquility are here within these walls—and in our hearts.

April 25 — home

We had a good Easter day. I got up early and hid about seventy eggs, in spite of the fact that the ground was sopping wet. We went to church, then out to Bill's folks' farm for dinner. Then after dinner all those great big high school and college kids (our kids and their friends) had a ball finding eggs and slopping around in the mud puddles at the creek bank.

The high point of my day was the quiet time alone just after dawn, hiding eggs, listening to the birds, touching the apple blossom buds, discovering nests full of real eggs—robins and ducks—thinking about that first resurrection morning, all new and clean and victorious.

June 27 — home

Where has the summer gone? This one has been so full, and yet so little time for play. I've been walking in the early mornings as much as I can, and I've been on another diet. I was alarmed to discover that I'd worked my way up to as much as I weighed when I was pregnant. I've lost ten pounds now, but that is a drop in the bucket to what I need to lose. Bill's lost even more than that, but I seem to be stuck in one place.

The pull of the earth is always downward, and the struggle to become has to be on the inside, because the outside goes eventually the "way of all flesh"—sagging, drying, wrinkling, decaying, and going about its process of "returning to the earth from whence it came."

This month has been full of people and events. The fiftieth anniversary celebration for Bill's parents went off without a hitch. Everything went right on schedule, and between one hundred fifty and two hundred people were here, I think. George and Lela couldn't believe the whole thing—especially the number of old friends who came from far away.

Everyone had a great time, especially Aunt Lillie (age ninety-one now), who "worked the crowd" like someone running for office.

July 31 — home

Uncle Jess died. I've never felt so certain that the body is left behind like a cicada shell on the bark of a tree. There was little sadness at the funeral home, and not even what outsiders would call "respect." People felt free to talk, even laugh, because no one seemed to feel that Jess was there or that death was there.

Uncle Jess had lived with joy and thankfulness a life of commitment to his Lord. His life had come to a natural and complete end in this time-space and had gone on to real Life somewhere else. We were just there to honor and celebrate a completed chapter and to christen and launch another. We were not doing it in his presence, but he'd left his body behind as a piece of memorabilia.

This is the death of a saint. It is as it should be.

August 3 — Traverse City, Michigan

The familiar smell of water and fish is erasing all the hours and months and years between now and other times I've spent beside the lakes and oceans of my life. My soul is home. The waters of Lake Michigan wave goodbye to this Friday in August as the sun begins to slip behind the pines that outline Traverse Bay.

Bill and I are alone, and we are still a bit unused to it. For all those years, children's voices and needs and laughter and arguments have been the norm. Sometimes we've longed for silence and privacy; this week there's been silence on demand and plenty of privacy and, as I said, it seems a little awkward sometimes.

But we'll learn again to be at home with silence and having each other alone. We drove all the way out to the lighthouse and Old Mission Peninsula. The whole peninsula is dotted with orchards and vineyards: peaches, red and black cherries, apples, and grapes. Then we found this inn by the water. We've eaten here before, but never stayed. All they had left was a lovely suite. But we are celebrating each other and the rest of our lives, so we splurged and took it.

August 4 ~ Traverse City

The lake is veiled (not shrouded) in mist; the far shore is barely visible and looks like a memory. The noisy gulls were the first ones here this morning, brazenly demanding some bread as if it were their due. Then came the mallards, timid not by nature, but by the gulls' intimidation.

And then appeared the subtle outline of a family of swans with three half-grown cygnets, slowly drifting into focus and reality. Without a sound or threat, they moved toward the congregation of lesser creatures, who parted to make room. The gulls made no protest; the mallards silently moved far into the background.

The protective hen stopped several yards from shore and hovered there with her three babies, while the regal cob came close, then returned to them. Then, with the cygnets between them, the pair drifted gracefully down the beach into the sunrise.

Today we will go to visit the "hometown" of my teenage years and attend my twenty-fifth class reunion. I wonder what memories will surface there. The years there were a kaleidoscope

of smooth and sharp edges, the pieces of glass that make up its designs are clear and colorful as well as clouded and opaque. With the cylinder of twenty-five years to peer through, I wonder if there will be any pattern to it all.

It doesn't really matter. I have Bill and our life together and our children. I have made my statement with the time I've been given, and I've nothing to prove or defend. Love has been good to me, so good that I've had plenty left over to give away.

So, give us this day.

September 5 — home

Benjy got his braces off today and feels as though he is all teeth. His new straight teeth have turned him into a handsome young man. He also has contacts, one of which he ruined last night by screwing it into the lid of his contact case. But mostly he's done pretty well with them and is enjoying being able to see.

This is the third day of Suzanne's sophomore year at college, and she seems so much more happy and confident this year. She couldn't wait for school to start this time, but was glad, too, to have the week in Nantucket just before beginning.

Tonight there were about one hundred kids and youth leaders here to kick off the school year for the church youth group. They had a great time playing and being together. Amy loved all the excitement and interaction, and Benjy seemed to be proud to have them here, too. It is a great, supportive group of young people. I praise God for their impact on our kids' lives, and for leaders who care enough to really get involved.

December 7 — Community Hospital, surgical waiting room

Surgery again, the second time in four weeks. The time passes so slowly—it takes days, it seems.

One hour. Two. The doctor comes at last. He is not alone. The second doctor, a family friend, does not look up; our eyes never meet.

The surgeon repeats well-rehearsed words: "Your mother did fine. The lesion was larger than we thought, about like this." (He gestures with his fingers and makes a circle to indicate the size of a silver dollar). "And . . ."

His sentence trails off. I search his face. It is boyish, earnest. "And there was some invasion of surrounding tissue maybe, we can't be sure. It was deep. The bladder, the bowel wall, maybe the uterus. We may need a few chemo treatments."

He makes excuses. "Old scar tissue from other problems. Could be other things, but it looks as if there may be some invasion of the walls."

We go back to wait in the narrow room and contemplate. Another cup of coffee. What will this mean?

A friend, a young father, the biology teacher at the high school, died like this two years ago last week. His daughter is Amy's friend. His cancer began in the bladder, then spread

until it devoured all there was of him—including, at the end,
his personality, so that after it was over, his family had to
struggle to recall his old self and to forget what had become
of him.

My sister and I sit silently. We contemplate the enemy, this
voracious monster who materializes inside someone you love and
begins to eat its way through the living organs until it has sucked
out all their normal function. Then one day it eats one that is
needed to sustain life. That is all.

George and Lela come to wait, and Bill's Aunt Maimie.
Family . . . when all there is to do is "be there." They are here
waiting, loving, talking about trivial things like the wind chill
and dog houses because they understand that the real things that
consume us now are too poignant to talk about.

Two hours and more. Past time for Mother to be taken from
recovery. We watch for familiar feet passing through the hallway
on a wheeled cot. She doesn't come.

The phone rings at the end of the hall. The receptionist comes
to the narrow room to say that Mother's blood pressure is
unstable. She must stay longer.

We wait. Another hour. Two.

At last they push past the narrow room a cart with a shape
and size that looks familiar. We follow. The orderly lifts her
from the cart to her bed. Every movement is an agony. Tubes
and plastic bags go with her everywhere.

In the room we sit and listen as small puffs of air pass her thin
lips. With each puff comes a small groan that cannot be uttered.
The pain is relentless, but the irregular blood pressure and low
body temperature tell us the body cannot risk another narcotic. So
we hold her hands, one of us on each side of her bed. . . .

Mother, I study your hands. I've memorized these hands for
forty years. There's the crooked fingernail that once was twisted
off in an old-fashioned washing machine wringer when you were
a child. The accident tore off the whole end of your finger, but
your mother taped it back on and commanded it to grow there

and it did. Your mother was a strong-willed survivor just as you are, as I am. All of us have hands that are far from cosmetic. Strong hands, utilitarian hands; hands veined from hard work, hardened by disinfectant and hot water, dried by weather and digging in the soil.

Your hands are cold. The shape and contours I've known so well are emphasized now by arthritis. They are like a cartoon caricature of the hands that taught me to cast a fishing line, curl hair, and smooth wrinkles. None of us have had the ivory hands of aristocracy—long, slender, smooth. No, we've worked too hard for that.

I remember Laura Oldham once said to me, "I've always wanted to paint a portrait of your hands." I started to feel complimented, for I've always wanted to have lovely hands. But then she went on. "They're not beautiful hands. No, they are rugged, utilitarian hands. They have—how shall I say?—character."

I knew she was right, and tried to content myself with having hands with "character" instead of beauty, but I've always wanted to have long, graceful hands with manicured fingernails. I would keep them, I think, flawlessly enameled and shaped.

Sometimes, when I'm on tour and there's nothing to do all day but read, watch my diet, and read, I grow long nails. It makes me feel like such a lady. But one week back at home's routine and I'm back to "character" hands again. Carol McSpadden, always an ivory lady, used to buy me manicure sets for Christmas, but I think she's long since despaired of trying to make a refined lady of me.

Amy, too, loves lovely hands and nails. When she succeeds in growing a nail or two, she paints it and files it and parades it before my eyes with pride. But before long, she's sure to "write" it off, or break it riding horses, or gouge it using it for a screwdriver to tighten the screws on her glasses or to fix the pads on her flute.

Amy, too, has servant hands. She, too, will have to settle for "character." These hands I hold, cold and gnarled—have character, seven and a half decades of it. Amy could do worse.

December 8 — hospital again

It was still dark when I got here. The snow crunched beneath my feet from the cold as I crossed the road from the parking lot to the hospital. The orderlies were readying things for the day; the recovering patients were being awakened for medicine and the night nurses were being replaced with rested help.

Mother was conscious. I say conscious rather than awake because she's had so much medication for pain. She floats in and out of awareness and often pauses at places in between, mixing events of yesterday with today and blending irrelevant worries with pressing concerns.

She's asking about Amy, about getting her to ballet, about taking back her library books on time. She talks about going to the bathroom though she has a catheter. And she asks about the malignancy—if the doctors told us more than he's told her. He has. I put her off.

She asks for water. I moisten her lips with a damp cloth.

And she wants me to fix her hair, though she's so drugged she can't force her hands to obey her commands to touch her head.

Evelyn comes. We clean Mother's teeth to make her mouth feel fresh and brush on some blush and eye shadow. She asks for a mirror, though her hands can barely grasp it. She wants to not look sick, but the convulsive contractions in her lower abdomen interrupt her efforts. She groans through five contractions—"Don't let me groan," she pleads. Then she sleeps, or rather drops behind the wall of unconsciousness. There is pain on her face; her brow is furrowed.

Evelyn goes to take her daughter, Lisa, to orchestra practice for the Christmas musical, "Cradle the King." Mother reaches for me. I cradle her. And the King becomes a child again, a child within a mother, cradled by a daughter.

December 11 — Mother's hospital room

Sounds in this room simulate order, dependability—the systematic ticking of the clock; the even, measured dripping of the sucrose and medication through the i.v. tube; the steady breathing as Mother sleeps. All seem ongoing, perpetual, and lull me into believing that the rhythm of life will go on.

The pathology report was encouraging, better than expected. Mother is better today, yet more aware of the pain . . . and of the future. Yet little things are getting easier—to turn in bed, to sit on the edge, to stand and walk with help to the door and back, a journey on which every step is a milestone. She is able to concentrate today, to follow and understand, to talk and crack a joke.

They bring her liquids: broth, apple juice, jello, tea. It has been five days. Her swollen tongue begins to regain its natural size and texture.

I read to her from Walter Wangerin's book, *Ragman*. This

chapter is a commencement address, and it is about learning to minister, trusting the promise of the power while one tarries in the city. In it, the church organist, a strong black woman of direct honesty, dies of cancer. I hadn't read it ahead of time. It is powerful and we both cry. Another minister comes to visit—the third today, but does not minister like the essay.

We are pleasant. He leaves, and Mother reads a bit from *The Saturday Evening Post,* then sleeps again. I write and read and feel guilty that I'm not writing the song Bill left for me to work on.

1985

Together the city and I start this day :
Lord, are you there ? In the streets ? In the faces ? In me ?

January 4 — home

I was caught in the whirlwind and swept through Mother's
homecoming, the preparations for Christmas, and the days of
celebration themselves. In my mind surface moments of excellence
and beauty: bringing Mother from the sterile hospital to the
warmth of Evelyn's home, all bedecked with Christmas; shopping
with Amy in the city on a school day; having Suzanne move
back into the nest for Christmas vacation, finding her asleep in
her room at night when I make my rounds; Bill and I celebrating
our anniversary in a favorite place, the whole evening and night
and morning stolen from the hectic pace to celebrate each
other; Christmas Eve with family, Christmas morning with
the dearest four in my life, Christmas afternoon with Evelyn's
family and Mother.

Bill did special giving this year—wonderful, impractical,
extravagant treasures to each of us: a leaded crystal
swan—graceful and diamondlike, for Amy; a lifelike, hand-done
sandcasting of a collie for Suzanne—a collie that looked
exactly like Pongo and nestled in a real cushioned dog basket;
a gold Olympic piece for Benjy. For me he'd found lovely
glass lanterns—cylinders that hold crystal oil lamps on
graceful glass rods, and he also gave me two absolutely
elegant outfits.

The kids had each done careful choosing with the money they
had to spend. It was a time of love and warmth. Christ was there
being celebrated with thoughtfulness and sacrifice.

God had given with extravagance Heaven's ultimate. And there
was a shadow of His loving abandonment there in our home, too.
Mother had marshaled all her energy and gone shopping—a
nearly impossible feat. She used her motorized chair to conserve
energy and drove herself to find the specific things she'd planned.

Her eyes danced with joy as we discovered and marveled at her achievement.

It was, in spite of everything—or maybe because of it—a Merry Christmas, full of joy and thanksgiving.

January 18 — home

Prayer has been needed for us this week, too, for me.

Benjy is at such a turbulent time—so conflicting, so many extremes in his personality just now. He's working so hard at learning and defining who and what he is. We are the buffers—the boundaries against which he is constantly bumping, crashing. Such a need for wisdom, we feel. How to be firm; how to be certain; how to be loving; how to be resilient, flexible; how to save the absolute for the absolutely important.

There was a crisis this week. Nothing overt, but an inner knowing that the spirit was on emergency alert.

Prayer. Urgent prayer. All the way to Waco in the night. Tears—unheard and unseen, hot and salty—spilling into the airplane blanket I was using to keep warm. The blanket was a boon: a sponge to absorb the tears, a silencer to muffle the sobs, a screen to hide the pain of having to leave just now.

Once again, as so many times before, the prayer was in groanings that I didn't know how to utter. It was a rebuke in Jesus' name of Satan—a binding. It was a claiming, a saving, a staking out claim for this precious child-man, so full of potential.

No wonder Satan wants him. What a prize he would be, what a trophy! "But I have prayed for thee."

At long last the weight of urgency lifted, and I slept in thanks for a power that knew no time/space/distance limitation. Yes, in the sky far above the southwest, God and I tucked a little boy into his bed in Indiana and wrapped him in the protection of the eternal. A mother tiptoed from his room in confidence and left him in better, more perpetual care. . . .

"And so it was that the days were accomplished that she should be delivered, and she wrapped him in swaddling clothes and laid him in a manger. . . ."*

Ever since, mothers have been wrapping their children in security blankets of eternal control and laying them in the feeding trough where they can be fed the "bread" that gives them eternal life and protected with the simple, even crude boards and planks of promise. And families go on finding shelter in caves of the spirit that the world does not notice or consider fitting, while others build their shelters of stone and mortar, line them with products and goods, embellish them with the glittering accessories of status.

" . . . and she kept all these things and pondered them in her heart."

January 27 – home

Tomorrow we will leave for Israel. Going with us will be about ninety singers from all over the country who have come together

*Luke 2:6, paraphrase of King James Version.

to be a choir. They will not know each other when we meet, but they all have in common that they know and have performed the musical, *He Started the Whole World Singing*. Many will bring spouses or family along, and together we will share what we expect to be some life-changing experiences.

We are to rehearse a few times with all the singers when we get there to get ready for the musical, which we plan to take as our gift to the Christian community that works and lives in and around Jerusalem. How we pray that this will be a time of binding together the body of believers who sometimes work in isolation and may be discouraged.

January 28 — in the air to Israel

This 747 is full of people headed for Israel. Many are with our tour group. One large group is teenagers who are involved in an exchange program with Israeli high schools. Others are Jewish people returning home or going to visit.

We go to build bridges, to try somehow to live down some of the atrocities that have been committed in the name of our Lord, to try to atone somehow by being as He taught. How far from His ways some have strayed in His name! How sad He must be, how He must have wept to see His own people treated in such appalling ways through the ages.

When we are mistreated, should that happen, I must remember the thick layer of distrust that has built up through the years.

When we left this morning, Suzanne was sick. It seems that it always happens that way: kids get sick when we can't be there to help. I went by to see her at her college dorm, took her a muffin and some milk, hugged her. How I hated to leave without her! It's the first overseas trip we've ever taken without her. I guess there is enough family left there to watch over her, but still . . .

The clock is beginning to catch up with me. Benjy and Amy are so tired. We will eat and then maybe sleep. It is 11:30 P.M. home time. In Israel it is 6:30 in the morning. No wonder we feel weary!

January 30 – Tel Aviv

The sun rose over a sand-colored city and glistened on the whitecaps of the beautiful Mediterranean Sea. Clear blue skies and an unseasonable sixty-five degrees. On the beach a young man is doing his morning yoga, standing on his head for long periods of time, then reciting his prayers.

We leave and start north, first to Jerusalem for a press conference. Good, tough questions are asked, and we do our best to answer honestly.

Our guide, Amir, is an intelligent young Jewish man, a political science major, member of the Labor party and a Zionist. He would like to be involved in government. Amir is a great resource person, not only for information about the sights, but for real content and insight into political and socioeconomic issues here.

We drive north toward Qiryat Shemona. On the way we see the Jordan Valley, now green and fertile; the desert; the wilderness; the Sea of Galilee. Then past the mountains of Moab, the land of the Philistines, and into the north part of the modern state of Israel, where the new settlements now sit in sentinel over the border.

Qiryat Shemona is a new town, built to defend the northern border and establish Israeli presence. The accommodations are simple, but the people are generous. Our group is given four motel rooms much like army barracks, for dressing, and a simple meal of chicken and vegetables.

The concert is in a theater, spartan and utilitarian, used for both films and community activities. Part of the audience is made up of soldiers in uniform, some with weapons resting in their laps. There are also people from the community and, of course, two hundred are our own tour group. Our people mingle in among the rest, which helps the concert because many of the local people do not speak English.

We are a little apprehensive at first, but we find the people to be responsive to the message and the music, especially the Israeli songs we have learned. Perhaps this concert is a start, an expression of the kind of love Jesus lived out here.

January 31 – Tiberias

Today we started from the glorious city of Tiberias on the Sea of Galilee. In contrast to yesterday, our room here is an extravagant suite provided by the tour company; it overlooks the clear and quiet waters. After a simple breakfast of breads, yogurt, cheeses, and fruits, we boarded a boat and sailed to the middle of the Sea of Galilee for a quiet time.

Today the Sea is calm and still. But at one end of the lake there is a cleft in the hills that, during storms, acts as a wind tunnel to churn these waters into a tempest with little warning. We stop in the center of the lake and turn off the motor. Sandi Patti sings "Stranger of Galilee." We read the account of Jesus speaking "Peace" to the waves. We sing "Alleluia," but wish for a song we all know that could express what we're feeling. There is none.*

We board our vehicles in silence and head north. We see the country of the northern kingdoms and its rugged beauty. We arrive at the Lebanese border at what is just now called the "Good Wall" where soon the troops will be withdrawn from Lebanon. The next few weeks will be interesting to watch. Chances are the PLO will come in again across the border.

We drive out to a place in the foothills of Mt. Hermon—a surprising oasis far from steamy Jerusalem where a natural spring gushes from the rock and then runs crystal clear along the basin below—the main source for waters of the river Jordan.

It seems that this was a vacation spot for dignitaries across the centuries of Palestinian history. We climb the rock to where once stood a Greek shrine to Pan, the god of nature. It was here, too, that Herod later built his lavish summer palace; this was the setting of the city called Caesarea Philippi, named by Herod in honor of Rome's Caesar Tiberius.

So it was here that the pagan Greeks and the affluent political coalition of Jewish leaders and Roman officials all came to

*This experience later gave birth to the song, "Peace, Be Still."

indulge their appetites and erect their magnificent symbols of earthly power.

But this was also the setting for Jesus' famous question to His disciples, "Who do you say that I am?"—to which Peter, the dullest and least insightful of the bunch, blurted out, "You are the Christ, the Son of the Living God."

Jesus, then, in the shadow of this rock used by earthly kingdoms, both political and religious, said to Peter, "This insight didn't come from you. It came from divine revelation. You are Peter [Jesus used the word *petros*, meaning a stone or pebble], but upon this rock [now he uses the word *petra*, meaning a solid bedrock or foundation] I will build my kingdom, and the gates of hell itself shall not prevail against it."*

Now, Jesus must have been playing with the words for "rock." He will not build his kingdom on this cool, aloof rock where one earthly empire gives way to more powerful ones, nor on a person who happens to be the recipient of insight, but on the solid foundation (how like Him to choose an invisible one) of "divine revelation." Armies could not march against it; governing bodies could not move or dissolve it; the powerful could not take it by force—but the simplest could possess it by faith.

How like Him—to always take the path the world would least understand or predict: a kingdom built on the unshakable foundation of divine revelation and simple faith in what is revealed.[†]

February 3 — Jerusalem

Today we went to visit a local congregation of Christians here in the city. Their church had been torched by extremists, so they were worshiping in a temporary building of corrugated steel and

---

*From Matthew 16:17–18, paraphrased.
[†]It was from this experience that the song, "Upon This Rock," grew.

plastic sheeting constructed on the remaining cement slab. The rain pounded down on the plywood roof while the wind whipped the plastic sheets that covered the doorways. Yet, to this accompaniment, they all sang and praised the Lord. There was much prayer for special needs and many words of encouragement.

One of the spontaneous choruses that was sung was, appropriately, "It's Beginning to Rain." Someone whispered the rumor that we had written the song and were present in the service.* So the song leader called Bill up to sing a verse and then sing a few other songs. Each time the people joined in on the choruses. It was an incredible experience to have our songs precede us to a foreign place.

Rain ran across the cement floor, but there was warmth and love running through our hearts and gratitude for a place, any place, to meet together as a body of believers to sing and grow strong for the tasks ahead:

> I have promised to pour my spirit out
> on your sons and your daughters;
> If you're thirsty and dry,
> look up to the sky
> It's beginning to rain.

February 4 — Jerusalem

The days and nights are so full there is no time to write. I must remember one experience, though, that happened in the hotel in Tiberias.

The directors had scheduled a room in the hotel where we could rehearse with the choir. But there was no piano in the room, so the hotel management told us we could rehearse in the lobby area, where several people were already sitting.

---

*Actually, we had written it with Aaron Wilburn.

First, we prayed together, asking God to bless our newly formed choir and to give us understanding of the work we were doing. Then Bill asked me to explain the overall message and intent of the musical.

So I began with the Garden of Eden and the perfect communion God had with all His creation, especially the human persons He'd made so like Himself. I talked about how everything was eternal and the word for that eternal quality of everything in harmony with God was "glory." But then man disobeyed, trading the eternal for the immediate, and the "glory" departed. Work became a chore, life came to know pain, and the days passed without a dream.

Then I explained about how, even then, God had a plan to buy us back, restore us to our original joy, and bring back the "glory"—about how He needed a people to keep alive the memory of a "better way," a people who could pass on to their children that life once knew "glory" and that God had promised to one day bring back the eternal to life.

Then the choir began to sing the words to "Bring Back the Glory," "Zion Kept On Calling through Their Tears," and "Next Time We Meet."

When we got through, an elderly Jewish man burst into tears. He came rushing up, threw his arms around me, and said, "Oh, thank you! Thank you for reminding us what we are all about. Sometimes we have forgotten; we have forgotten!"

That night those ninety separate strangers from different American churches became a single organism, a real body of believers, joined by the "song" that started in that very country on a Judean hillside long ago, a song that had the power to put the music back into all our days.

February 8 — Jerusalem

What can I say about these experiences for which there are no words?

The musical concert with the Christians of Israel was an experience I shall never forget. Five hundred Christians from all kinds of ethnic and denominational backgrounds crowded into the Jerusalem Hilton ballroom. The choir sang as if they had worked together for months. Sandi, Cozette Byrd, Jon Mohr, Gary McSpadden, Larnelle Harris, Bill and I had such an incredible time sharing with this audience that it was difficult to speak and sing. Perhaps the best of all was to see all these believers take Communion together, celebrating the broken body of our Lord who walked this very city on His way to His death to "bring back the glory" into each of our lives.

We had stood together in the dungeon where He was imprisoned; we had walked the Via Dolorosa, the Way of Sorrows; we had stood on the hill called the "place of the skull," with its sunken eye sockets overlooking what is now an Arab bus depot but what had once been the city dump; and together we had sung "Because He Lives I Can Face Tomorrow" at the empty tomb in the quiet garden.

Now we served the wine and the bread to these who were eternally joined to us because of His finished plan to buy us all back, restore us to the Eden of our souls.

I breathed a prayer of thanks that Amy and Benjy were in this place, filled with these experiences—and a prayer of thanks for all of the children and young people who had walked with us here.

February 27 — back home, the cabin

I'm trying to write. I wonder how many entries have begun that way. I am so segmented I must resemble an earthworm in my soul.

Whenever I get serious about blocking out time to write, everyone seems to think that is a signal to give me things to write. So I either have to just make them mad and come off sounding selfish or let my time be filled up with other projects and get no closer to my goals than if I'd never tried! Bill wants

me to work on a dozen songs (at least!), Gary wants me to write a promo campaign for the Vocal Band's new album. Our promotion people want plans for the Dove Awards reception. And always there are important letters to write.

But I (is it selfish?) want to write a book about the generation of women I live in and about the generation on each side of me. I want to see Mother's and Suzanne's and Amy's poetry in print, and I want to say things about women that no one in the Christian community is saying.

Besides all these writers at war in me, there are other selves to contend with. As mother of Amy, I need to give her extra guidance and presence just now. Dating is new and exciting for her, yet she feels it driving a wedge between us. What she really feels is the conflict between wanting independence and wanting protection and nurture. Time is a tyrant for her, too, and there isn't enough of it to give all of her relationships top priority. Something always gets cheated and guilt ensues. Welcome to womanhood, Amy.

And Benjy is a top priority just now. Still a little boy, yet also a man in the bud, showing great encouraging signs of maturing. I see him moving into the time when he and Bill will become great friends. Men together.

Suzanne, too, calls for large chunks of me. More independent than ever, yet needing constant reinforcement and a sure sounding board for her thoughts.

Bill and I long for more time for intimacy—perhaps so much brokenness around us makes this even more imperative. We run to each other for security, yet have so many demands on our time. We need more time for each other.

Mother is well now, except for her leg,* and wants to do things. How I love to fiddle away days with her and Evelyn, visiting antique shops, buying spring flowers to plant, doing all sorts of things as an excuse for being together. We are all there is of our family, and we are treasuring our time together just now.

And we have a new computer. I need to learn word processing. When? Where do I get the hours it takes to learn the things that would save me so much time? One more voice to scold my conscience.

Next weekend I speak in Oklahoma. Last weekend it was Portland, and this Saturday the Leighton-Ford breakfast. I love speaking, too, and need preparation time to do a good job.

I must stop writing in this journal now to write on one of these projects. I just needed to paint this signpost along the roller-coaster road of my emotions.

March 8 — plane to Oklahoma City (for speaking engagement)

I don't seem to have learned in these forty-three years to be resigned to my limitations or at ease with the frustrating snail's pace with which I'm able to dole out my ideas.

My mind is the Atlantic Ocean dammed up behind a towering concrete wall, with only a thimble-sized hole through which the flow is allowed to escape. There are always too many thoughts, too many insights, too many questions.

*Mother had also had a full knee replacement.

I know others look at what I've written in my span and read off the statistics accompanied by adjectives like "prolific" and "productive." But to me the poems and song lyrics have been droplets that have been allowed to escape through my time schedule, opportunity, and place in history, giving only a hint of the gush that lies still trapped.

Sometimes the wall has been a blessing, forcing me to distill the thoughts into a crystal drop of purity and clarity, since it will be all that is allowed to represent the whole. Other times, I feel as though the wall will not hold—that it will be crushed to pieces and carried away by the thrust of all that churns unseen.

Sometimes my mind digs little rivulets to let the force of it all drain off a bit, creating little side streams to bypass the wall and keep it from exploding. These trips are one such side stream, and I'm thankful for it.

May 1 — spring tour, Toronto

We made it home for just long enough to realize that we needed to stay, that our kids needed us to stay, that mother needed me to stay, and everything that distinguishes me from the animals needs me to stay . . . at home.

But we said "goodbye" again and left for Kankakee Nazarene College and here. The college students were enthusiastic last night, and that was a blessing because we were so low about leaving home yet one more time. We floated through the concert buoyed by their exuberance and once more found restoration in reaching out. I'm sure, though, that the audience gave us more than we gave them, and that in exchange they themselves were fed. Sometimes bread cast upon the water is stale and dry and needs the moisture that only a good wave-tossing can bring.

Benjy is not happy about our being gone, though he doesn't say so the way the girls do. All of them, I think, have felt the conflict between wanting us to keep doing what we do and having that "bottom's-dropped-out" feeling when we're gone.

May 11 — home

Tomorrow Suzanne and I leave for the trip to New York City and Washington, D. C., that will let us see where the needs are in the inner city and how God is at work there. It is a part of a class we're both taking—Suzanne for college credit, me for graduate credit.

This is the worst possible time for me to go, since we just got back from tour, yet I have felt so driven to do this. I know this experience will change our lives and our writing, and experiencing it together will be unforgettable. We pray that nothing will keep us from being open to what God wants to teach us.

We will fly out late together so we can spend as much time at home as possible. The college group will drive in a van.

May 12 — in the air on the way to New York

This morning Suzanne and I left early (7:00 A.M.) to begin our trip. What will come of this—what it will call us to—is unknown, frightening, and somehow exciting.

I have a feeling this trip is somehow tied to the unsettled feeling we've had that God is leading us once more into something new. God is getting us ready for something. I hope we have the sense to know just what and the willingness to obey when we see it.

We arrived safely and took a cab to the Vanderbilt YMCA. It is a clean and adequate facility right in the heart of the city. After everyone got settled, we went for a walking tour of the city, ate at a deli-pizza sort of place, and then walked some more.

I called home. Benjy played bass in church tonight for a special group to sing "Fully Alive." Then he and Bill went to get fish and chips. Mother's Day. They had taken the Mother's Day plants and notes to both our mothers, too, then they ate yogurt for lunch. I hope they survive until I get home.

May 13 — New York

Across from the "Y" there is a little place called The Deli Place where I've come for coffee and a bran muffin. It is 7:30 A.M., so except for a few workers of the city, I'm alone. The radio station is playing "She Believes in Me." The place is like hundreds I've seen before—small, nondescript community place where there is warmth and familiarity to escape the loneliness for a while and hear other human voices talking—friendly voices who sound comfortable with each other.

This is a student area, a street of young pilgrims from every country—hopefuls looking for the promise of the land of milk and honey. ("Hello. I'm from Spain. I just got here. . . .")

Across the street, a blue-shirted worker lights up a cigarette before going into one of the many garages or street construction places for his day's occupation. Delivery trucks squeeze through the tiny arteries of the city, bringing supplies and nourishment to its sinew and bone.

Outside our entry into the "Y" is a pile of sand that has been dumped for construction. Someone has put work shoes at the end of the pile, hands and a bouquet of plastic flowers at the head to make it look as if someone is buried there. An inflated condom protrudes from the peak of the sand, and an obscene epitaph is printed on the "headstone."

On the rooftop below the room where I am staying are strewn pornographic magazines and obscene graffiti. Skin shops abound in a few blocks . . . but so do grand old churches (like St. Peter's) and Bloomingdale's, Bergdorf Goodman's, and the Chase Manhattan Bank.

In my heart, I bring my world with me to this place: my children, Bill, my Mother and her pain, our extended family and its problems, our hopes, dreams, disappointments, and failures.

Together the city and I start this day: Lord, are you there? In the streets? In the faces? In me?

May 14 — New York

My mind and feet are overworked and a little sore this morning—so many miles, so much information, and so many needs.

Yesterday we met with Dale Stoltzfus of the Mennonite Church in Harlem, who discussed some of the basic "givens" in working in the inner city and how a Christian could hope to affect it. He

seemed very committed and focused in his mission and belief in Jesus as the power to change things. He seemed to have in perspective the necessity of alleviating people's suffering and fighting for justice as ways to express Jesus to people in a tangible way to point them to a freedom that can only be known when spirits are liberated.

May 17 — New York

This has been a good week with Suzanne. I admire her as a person who has a good heart and sharp mind. I'm excited about all that is happening in her life.

Each person in this group seems to have something unique to bring. There is almost perfect harmony among us, and a deep commitment to understanding and acceptance. Gradually all of the small differences in the group are giving way to understanding and a singleness of purpose.

Yesterday morning we were at St. John the Divine Episcopal Church at 7:00 A.M. for a communion service. The church is in the process of building an enormous addition. They have brought in stone cutters to teach this vanishing art to unemployed inner-city dwellers. The model for each figure to be engraved in stone is first sculpted of clay, and the stone carvers work from this clay sculpture. It would be interesting to do a book about what the experience of working on the church, carving the saints, will do to the lives of these artists, many of whom will not live to see the construction completed.

On Thursday afternoon we took the subway to a section of Brooklyn, the most hostile area we have encountered on the whole trip. There was much destruction along the streets from vandals and disrepair. Clumps of restless black youths eyed us from street corners, and school children walking home registered open resentment at our being in their neighborhood. It was quite a walk through this atmosphere to Rev. Johnny Ray Youngblood's church. But we got there safely, and security let us into the church to wait for someone to speak to us.

The things believers in this area have accomplished are phenomenal. The various churches have joined forces to deal with their common problems. Working together, they have used legal coercion and just plain hard work and persistence to force City Hall into doing in Brooklyn what needed to be done: replace street signs, upgrade grocery stores, and grant zoning to build one-family housing. These housing units were built by a retired contractor with financing from the coalition of churches and various other groups for half what the government could build for. Nehemiah Plan, as all this has come to be called, has become a model for the nation of what can be done to redeem decaying neighborhoods.

May 20 — ONE Ministry, Washington, D.C.

Today we served at the breakfast for the street people provided by a caring group of lay people who love the homeless and have come to know them by name. We served any way we could—setting tables, cooking, or cleaning up. Some of us led the worship time with the men and women before they ate.

Then we went to Howard University to hear Calvin Morris. A sort of strange thing happened. I asked him to tell us if there was any use preparing for a caring ministry if we were always going to be suspect just because we were white. He began to answer, then said, "Well, there's a song that is often sung at Easter, but I like to sing it all year. It goes, 'Because He Lives I Can Face Tomorrow.' I have to think life is worth the living if we're real. Not easy, but worth it. . . ."

Everyone was saying things and making gestures. He thought he'd said something wrong. Finally, the students let him know that I had written the words he was quoting. I was embarrassed, he was somewhat flustered, and the kids got a big laugh out of it all.

May 21 – Washington, D.C.

So many things I've learned as we've walked the streets of these two great cities: I've come to know the street people and the homeless not as faceless members of a sociological phenomenon, but as real individuals needing a place to belong.

I've learned that they are not who we often think they are—most are the helpless and vulnerable, the powerless and the broken.

Some have been released from mental institutions because they were too "well" to be there, but they are no match for the streets or the system.

Some are educated and brilliant, but have failed or given up somewhere along the way and were too broke to go home and too ashamed to ask for help.

Some are unskilled, and in a time when even unskilled jobs are being done by skilled labor, there is no work for them to do.

Some were victimized by pimps and porno kings when they

were children and spit back out on the streets when they were no longer of use to that sick, perverted industry.

One inescapable truth nags at me from the pages of Scripture: God identifies not with the rich and powerful, but with the poor and disenfranchised. He calls all who follow Him to be servants. We must start right where we are, but we must not limit ourselves to the needs we feel most comfortable with.

There are so many places to serve that no one can escape the crying need. I saw one person serving by cutting the toenails of those who are too old and too stiff from the cold and from arthritis to cut their own. The nails had grown out, curled around and grown back into the bottom of the toe. Walking the streets with toenails poking into the toes causes infection and pain, and sometimes feet have to be amputated to prevent the spread of infection. So one servant felt called to cut toenails.

A young dentist gave his time pulling decayed teeth. A young attorney helped the powerless fill out welfare forms, establish a mailing address, and cut through the mind-boggling red tape of bureaucracy. Still others fried eggs in the morning or passed out sandwiches at night near the grates in the city streets where the homeless gather in the winter to absorb what warmth may come up from the pipes below the city.

Another sight remains with me. Lucite boxes about the size of a child's shoebox and half-filled with what looked like gray sand lined the top of an old upright piano in the parlor of the house that was home to the Center for Creative Non-Violence. There was a name on each box. "What are these?" I had naïvely asked. "Those are the ashes of persons who froze or died in the street last winter. No one knew them; no one claimed them. There was no identification. We thought they needed to die with a name, an identity. Christ would have us give them that, at least. So here they have names. Here someone remembers."

Now we must go home and live this all out where we are.

And . . . we must try to put into words for our professor "where we saw Christ at work in the city" . . .

May 23 — home

> I walked today where Jesus walked,
> And felt His presence there . . .

Bethlehem, Galilee, Gethsemane—He walked there. But today
Christ walks the concrete sidewalks of Times Square, 47th Street,
and Broadway. And as He walks, His feet are soiled—not with the
sand of the seashore or the reddish dust of the Emmaus Road, but
with the soot and filth of the city.

He walks the "Great White Way," and His face is lit by the
gaudy neon signboards of materialism. He walks in the shadows
of the dark alleyways, where faces are not lit at all.

He walks with children and goes where they are taken when
they are enticed and bartered to gratify some sick perversion. He
walks the steaming hallways of welfare hotels, where mothers cry
themselves to sleep in worry and despair.

He does not sleep, but lies beside the broken in their
vermin-infested shelters and hears the homeless groan in their

delirium; He walks between the bodies as they wake, touching heads of matted hair, offering a hand to lift the men and women who are stiff from lying on the drafty floor.

He walks the streets of Harlem and Chinatown, Brooklyn and the Bronx, and stops to stand with those whose buildings smolder, whose sons are lost to drugs, whose mothers are evicted, whose daughters sell their bodies for a meal.

He walks the subway aisles offering His seat to the old, the weary, the pregnant. He is jostled with the throngs at rush hour and reads the signs that offer satisfaction from Jack Daniels or a hot line to call to rid one's body of a growing life.

He is pushed and shoved through Grand Central Station, elbowed and ignored, yet in the crowd He feels a measure of virtue flow from His being and searches through the faces for an honest seeker passing by.

Christ walks the city. I've seen him there. I've seen His blistered, broken feet, galled by the shoes without the socks. He walks the city on children's feet that grow too fast to stay in shoes at all. He walks the street in high-heeled shoes that pinch the toes but attract the client.

He walks the city. He stands behind a table serving breakfast, drives a truck that carries sandwiches to the grates where homeless sleep to garrison themselves against the cold. He climbs the narrow staircases of burned-out buildings and restores them into homes again. He paints and disinfects and hauls out trash.

I've seen Christ stand by a dental chair fixing worn-out teeth. I've seen Him tutoring a dropout and heard Him say, "Keep reaching for the sky." Christ holds a baby whose mother is a child herself, so needing to be mothered—and holds that mother's mother in His arms at night when prayers become such groanings that they cannot be uttered. He groans with them all—a mother to three generations of the motherless.

Christ walks the city and carves saints in stone for some cathedral—the cherubim and seraphim with faces of the street.

He weaves the cloth that transforms rags into a lovely tapestry. Christ dances when He Himself can find no other way to say "'I love you" to a world in which there is left no word for "Love." He acts the part that tells the story of how that Love invaded humankind, for only story tells the Story. Christ incarnate. Christ the living, walking parable, takes to the stage to be the Story.

Christ the advocate walks the city. "You have an advocate with the Father," He said. That is done. But now the powerless need an advocate with the government—to help with the red tape, the powers-that-be. Christ walks there. Jesus, "our lawyer in heaven," walks the city to become a lawyer in the streets—filling out welfare forms, phoning caseworkers, petitioning agencies, drafting legislation to protect the poor. Christ the Advocate walks the city.

Christ walks the city's Ivy Halls where students debate His existence. He holds out his nail-scarred hands to the agnostics and invites them "touch and see." He is there at the "gay caucus" and the "feminist rally" and the meeting for the "apartheid demonstration." He who is question and answer, He who sets brother against brother, yet whispers "peace, be still" to the turbulent waves, walks here.

Christ walks the halls of government, and in His presence statesmen hammer out the laws. The just and the unjust, the honest and the ruthless, those who struggle for truth and those who live the lie convene in His presence, for Christ walks the marble halls of government, sifting the "wheat from the chaff."

Christ walks the corridors of justice. He is in night court and stands with the accused and the accuser. He who is truth and mercy and justice weighs them both and walks both to the judge's chamber and the prisoner's cell.

Christ is no stranger to locks and bars. He paces with the convicted her narrow space and hears the curses of despair. Yes, Christ is present in the prisons, where fear has built walls around the heart thicker than the walls that guard against escape and higher than the barbed wire that makes an ugly frame for the gray skies. He walks the empty corridors and offers the key of freedom to whomever would become citizens of a new country, a different kingdom. It is the very key He offers to the judge who is also a captive, a key that makes both the sentencer and the condemned free men and women—family.

Christ calls all to Communion. The table of the Eucharist is spread. He takes the bread. He is the Bread. He breaks it, breaks Himself, and offers this brokenness to us, explaining that if we take it, we ourselves must be broken and consumed. He takes the cup. It is the pouring out of Himself. He says, "Won't you, too, be poured out with me?"

The table is long and spans centuries. Some leave the table to go in search of silver. Some chairs were empty from the start, for though many were invited some had wives to marry, parents to bury, houses to build, empires to manage.

Those who have come are a motley blend of ages and nationalities, races and genders. But they are all poor and hungry and needy. Slowly, they break the bread—again and again—and lift their morsels to their mouths. It does not go down easily. Sometimes it sticks in the throat . . . until the wine is passed. The pressed and poured-out fruit washes away the dryness.

The bread—"My flesh"—and the wine—"My life's blood"—together make a sacrament of joy, and the rite becomes a celebration of paradox. In the breaking we have become whole. In the pouring out, we have been filled. In bringing our poverty and hunger and need, we have been made rich. In daring to sit with seekers whose differences we did not understand, we have been made one.

Christ the paradox walks the city. He is the broken, and He is the healer. He is the hungry, and He is the Bread of Life. He is the homeless, yet it is He who says, "Come to Me all you who are overloaded, and I will be your resting place." He is the loser who makes losing the only way to win. He is the omnipotent who calls all who follow to choose powerlessness and teaches us how by laying down all power in heaven and in earth. He is the sick, and He is the wholeness. He who said, "I thirst," is Himself the Living Water that promises we will never thirst again.

Just as the disciples in the Emmaus house recognized their Lord through the broken bread and the shared cup, so our blindness turns to sight in Holy Communion, and we see Him for who He truly is.

1986

I know that my doing is of dwindling value
when there is no space for silence.

January 4 – home

This day is for silence.

So many voices call to me, "No, there is no time! You must spend this day doing!"

But I know that my doing is of dwindling value when there is no space for silence. Speaking is no good without first listening to what was spoken into the space of the Beginning. Words are drained of their meaning when there is no focus on the Word that *is*, that was in the space of the first silence, quiet yet insistent.

And how can *I* start a new year without attention to silence and an inward journey into space—the space within myself, the space without. It is space that traces around me, like a child traces around her hand on a clean page of paper, separating what is me from the throng of other souls in this crowded anthill of earth. Without the space, I would blend into the masses and in time forget that I am.

January 18 – home

I'm a nest builder, and privileged among nest builders because human nests are portable. While birds must collect the fibers of their habitat and weave them to a rooted branch for their security, I carry the golden threads of joy in bags and satchels and weave them upon arrival around the strong framework of loving relationships—so home is wherever we are together.

I've built nests on airplanes, in motel rooms, on buses, in cabins, under shade trees, by campfires, in dressing rooms, and behind stage curtains. A few books, some crayons, a soft blanket, pencils and paper, a coffeepot, some table games, familiar toys, some peanut butter and crackers—and some impersonal place becomes our safe refuge into which we snuggle and hide from the world.

Today we fly and will build a nest tonight on board a ship in the Caribbean. Give me thirty minutes and my satchel, and I will transform a cabin into a place to roost safely and incubate ideas and relationships. Soothing lotion on the night stand, good books and magazines by the chair, tablets and pencils on the desk, music and a tape player, soft slippers and some fruit—and the fledglings will find a place of security and warmth where their growing can go on without an interruption.

February 2 – home

This morning Benjy couldn't find anything to wear to church. Suddenly his sweaters were all too tight, his pants were too short, his jackets were too skimpy, and his shirts didn't feel right. The shoestring broke in his new deck shoes, and besides he had a fever blister when he woke up.

"Just go without me," he said through his swollen lip. "I'll look too awful for you to go with me." I put my arms around his big, strong shoulders, but the tears in his eyes betrayed the little boy inside.

"I know how you feel," I said. "Sometimes my body just won't go into last year's clothes, and nothing works. It's all right, though, for you. You're just growing; you can't help it. And when you get through, you're going to be so proud of your body!"

Together we looked through his closet and sorted through the mound of slacks and sweaters already on his bed. He was right; only one pair of pants was big enough, and those were the very ones he'd worn for the last three weeks.

"I can't wear these again, Mother!" There was all the confusion of adolescence in his face—all the longings for me, for someone, to understand without his having to say it how much it means to a boy to feel acceptable, to look "cool," to be confident that he is worthy.

And I knew. I knew that no child should have to feel self-conscious and preoccupied about something as transient as clothes. I remembered how good it felt to be able to forget myself and be myself because I wasn't embarrassed about how I looked. Soon, I knew, this little boy would be a real man and have real skills and real abilities and would know himself enough to not worry about the confidence-building properties of clothes. But not yet, not yet.

Benjy didn't need a guilt trip about getting ready for church on time or appreciating what he had. He only needed understanding without explanation, acceptance when he couldn't accept himself, and a deep knowing that he was truly loved in this house.

Oh, yes—and he needed something to wear to church.

Together we discovered that if we put his same black and gray pants with his new blue-striped shirt and the pale yellow sweater vest he got for Christmas, no one would notice that the pants were the same ones he'd worn all winter and for the last three Sundays. I fixed his shoestring by tying some knots in the lace, and I promised to stay and wait with him while he got ready.

"But Dad's waiting!" he said.

"It's all right. If he needs to go on, I'll come with you and we'll drive," I told him. And I also promised, "Next week, we'll go shopping together, so you can choose the things that make you feel the best."

"Can we go to Castleton, not just to Anderson?" he asked.

"Sure can."

By now he had it all together; he just needed to brush his teeth. I ran on out to the car where Bill was waiting.

"Don't say a thing," I warned him. "Growing up is hard some days, and this is one of those days." I choked on the rest of what I might have said, but Bill knew. He'd been an awkward boy once, a boy from the farm who didn't have the "right stuff" to wear when it mattered. He knew.

When Benj came out, he looked great, and even better when Bill reached over the back of the seat to squeeze his knee and throw a grin in his direction.

"So much for being early, Dad." Benj said.

"Maybe next Sunday." Bill answered with pride in his voice.

February 15 – in the air over Denver

Flight home. I cram all I can into flight hours: reading, listening to tapes, writing. There is some turbulence here over Denver, though the sky is clear and sunny. The ground is brown with February, and there are white strips of snow down the crevices of the mountain. Geometric markings of farms and urban layouts carve the face of the valley, but as we move out these give way to the creative free-form of rambling rivers, softly curved hills, and subtle shadings of umber and toast. The sun catches the glassy surface of ponds and creeks to flash blinding rays back at us as we cross.

The Denver Nuggets were on the first half of the flight. A young boy about Benjy's age (fifteen) kissed his mother goodbye in Phoenix, then boarded the plane alone. He is excited about standing beside six players nearly seven feet tall, but has no one to share his excitement or to be impressed that he has rubbed shoulders (well, not *shoulders* exactly) with famous celebrities.

Bill and I put on earphones and listen to a young Jewish Christian sing on a tape. She sings "Jerusalem of Gold"—and high above Colorado we walk the streets of the old city and smell the marketplace. Amazing—the memory.

I think about how thankful I am to have been able to stuff so much into our children's memory banks. I know forgetting is not possible for them. They have *become,* and that cannot be taken away.

February 15 – home

I want to give our children the gift of solitude, the gift of knowing the joy of silence, the chance to be alone and not feel uncomfortable. I want to give them transportation for the inner journey and water for their desert places. I want to make them restless with diversion and disenchanted with the artificial excesses of our culture. I want to give them a desire to strip life to its essentials and the courage to embrace whatever they find there.

I would teach our children to be seers, to notice subtleties in nature and people and relationships. I long for them to grasp the meaning of things, to hear the sermons of the seasons, the exhortations of the universe, the warnings of the wounded environment.

I would teach them to listen. It would bring me joy to happen in on them and find them with their ears to the earth or humming the melody of the meadow or dancing to the music of the exploding symphony of spring.

Yes, I would teach them to dance! I would teach them never to so tie up their feet with the shackles of responsibility that they can't whirl to the rhythm of the spheres. I would have them embrace the lonely, sweep children into their arms, give wings to the aged, and dance across the barriers of circumstance buoyed by humor and imagination into the ecstasy of joy. I would teach them to dance!

I would teach our children to cry, to feel the pain that tears at the violated, to sense the emptiness of the deserted, to hear the plaintive call of the disoriented and understand the hopelessness of the powerless. I would teach them to cry—for what is locked away or broken, for what was not realized, for those who never knew Life, for the least and the last to know freedom.

I would teach our children gratitude. I would have them know the gift of where they've been and who brought them to where they are. I would teach them to write each day a liturgy of praise to read to the setting sun. I would have them dwell upon the gift of what is, not wasting their energies on what could have been.

And I would have them know that twin of gratitude, contentment. I would have them be content to live and breathe, to love and be loved, have shelter and sustenance, to know wonder, to be able to think and feel and see. To always call a halt to senseless striving—this I would teach our children.

I would teach our children integrity, to be truthful at any cost, to be bound by their word, to make honest judgments even against themselves, to be just, to have pure motives. I would have them realize that they are accountable individually to God alone and to themselves. I would have them choose right even if it is not popular or understood—even by me.

I would teach our children to pray, knowing that in our relationship with God there is much to be said and God is the one who must say it. I would have them know the difference between prayer and piety and make them aware that prayer often has no words, but only an open, vulnerable accessibility to God's love, mercy, grace, and justice.

I would hope that they discover that prayer brings and *is* an awareness of our need, a knowledge without which there is no growth or becoming. I would have our children know through experience and example that there is nothing too insignificant to lay before God. And yet I would have them learn that often, when we come to Him, He lifts us up until the matter we brought before Him seems insignificant compared to the revelation He brings to us.

I would not have our children think of prayer as a commercial enterprise, a sort of celestial clearinghouse for distributing earth's material goods. Rather, I would have prayer teach them that what we so often think we seek is not on the list of what we need, yet that God does not upbraid us for our seeking but delights in our coming to Him, even when we don't understand.

Mostly I would have our children know how synonymous true prayer is with gratitude and contentment and have them discover the marvelous outlet prayer is for communicating this delight with God.

Last, I would teach our children to soar, to rise above the common yet find delight in the commonplace, to fly over the distracting disturbances of life yet see from this perspective ways to attack the knotty problems that thwart people's growth and stymie their development. I would give them wings to dream and insight to see beyond the now, and I would have those wings develop strength from much use, so that others may be borne aloft as well when life becomes too weighty for them to bear.

At last these wings, I know, will take our children high and away from our reach to places we have together dreamed of. And I will watch and cheer as they fade from my view into vistas grand and new, and I will be glad.

February 25 — Charlotte, North Carolina

Prince—our precious little dog who has glued us all together and made the persons in our house better—Prince is dead. Bill's dad came in after the concert to tell us that he had been hit on the highway.

How can I say how we feel about losing Prince? He has been

such an unusual dog . . . sent to us, I think, because we needed him to help us all say the things that are hard for us to say to each other. He has brought us all closer and taught us patience with each other.

How strange that a little dog had to be there to help us communicate and care about each other. A little dog. . . . And we hug the dog and bathe him and laugh when he meets us at the door with his sock in his teeth or chomps down on his squeak toys to entice us to play.

We won't be the same. But no love is wasted . . . and a little dog gave us more than one speeding motorist could ever take away.

March 2 — Orlando, Florida

I think of home and the kids. And I dread walking in through the kitchen door and not finding that eager black-and-white face, sock in teeth, waiting to play and welcome us home.

I dread the walk with Benjy down the hillside where Prince bounded a week ago anticipating the awakening of spring . . . down, now, to the little place behind the hedge where the Indiana clay will be piled fresh over his little grave.

But it will be good to be home, and all this is a part of it . . . life, death, joy, pain, sharing the homecomings and the goodbyes. All are threads we carefully weave in the fabric of our days together, for we are a family.

March 14 — home

"When thou prayest, enter into thy closet, and when thou hast shut thy door, pray to thy Father which is in secret . . ."*

*Matthew 6:6, KJV.

In the life of a woman there is no closet where one can be in secret. I can't even get alone in the bathroom! Families are social institutions where there is always (or should be) interaction and lots of noise. Any mother knows that this scripture does not refer to a literal closet.

My closet I carry with me, and I am thankful that I can retreat into that inner sanctum of myself and close the door. In the yard, by the creek, in the car, at the sink, in the classroom, at my desk, on the plane, early in the morning, late at night, I duck into my closet, turn my back to the cacophony of sound, and face the silence. There I find the Father waiting, and in our secret place we both whisper, lest someone hear us and ask to join us there.

March 15 — home

They're remodeling the mall. Folding chairs in a sterile row replace the cozy "park benches"—yet the chairs are full, even an hour before opening time.

The mall is the "country store" meeting place of the computer age, for—computers or no computers—human beings will have, must have, community. So here, out of the weather, they gather. Some come to walk, recovering from heart bypasses, leg injuries, and love amputations.

"My God!" exclaims the young, virile man operating the coffee stand in the center. "Looks like the parade of the wooden soldiers!" He takes for granted his legs, his heart, and his relationships, unaware as yet of the fragility of life. An old man drinking coffee alone in the corner booth ignores his careless statement, pretending that he's hard-of-hearing instead of hurting.

The ladies smoke, but their conversation is their real smokescreen. They discuss the neighbors, the schools, the garage mechanics, the government, their weariness with the weather. But never, never do they mention what drives them

from their houses so early and into the warmth of some kind
of fellowship.

April 30 — flight to Phoenix

Flying to Phoenix for another leg of tour. Everything seems
overshadowed by the huge nuclear accident at Chernobyl in
the Soviet Union.

Yesterday it rained, normally a welcome shower for seeds I've
planted and asparagus roots and bulbs I've put out, but yesterday
I was suspicious of the rain and wondered if it carried to the earth
lethal doses of radioactive isotopes.

Today we fly. I love flying, but today I wonder if the turbulence
we are feeling is caused by the disturbance of the atmosphere or
whether the clouds we pass through are harboring cancer-causing
particles that will cling to the aircraft or fall to the green farms
below.

It is not that I fear death. I am very aware that this world is not
our home and that total annihilation will only bring us sooner to
"perfection." Yet I grieve for this earth, for nature, for the place
God wanted it to be. I sometimes wonder if an atomic burnoff is
the purging that will bring the "new earth," a place for our own
purged selves to enjoy another Eden of the eternal.

Meanwhile there is nothing to do but go on living, grateful
for the framework of routine that ushers us on through another
day—going to school, making appointments, leaving on tour,
doing the concert, working on the new hymnal, studying for
finals, moving home from the dorm, planting seeds, opening
the pool, eating dandelion greens, riding bikes, buying
graduation gifts, planning new projects, crowding three extra
kids around the supper table, enjoying sex and touching, going
to church . . . living with affirmation in the shadow of the
question.

May 5 — Fresno, California

I'm in a tiny coffee shop now writing, observing, and having coffee. A darling little blonde-headed boy about five years old runs up to me, puts his arms around me, lays his head on my

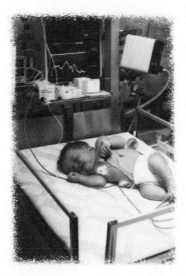

chest, and then dashes off to play with his little sister. His mother stands talking to another young woman and doesn't notice. The little boy must come from a very open, affectionate family; he seems to have developed no fear and no suspicions.

I wonder what a child would be like if he could grow to be a man without experiencing hurt or disappointment. Often I've wondered what children would be like in heaven. Do they stay the same age or do they go on growing there? Would a three-year-old killed by a car or an infant who died soon after birth or an aborted baby stay the same, or would they develop?

Maybe the answer is that children are able to grow on there, yet keep their open trust and never, never experience pain. What would such a perfect person be like? And will we all be transformed to such perfection—not only our bodies, but our emotions and psyches as well? No wonder Thornton Wilder said that every baby is "nature's attempt to make a perfect human being"!

May 22 — in the air over Indiana

After a long photograph session in Nashville, I left on the plane for home. It was just Steve, the pilot, and me; Bill had stayed to work with the Vocal Band album.

We had just taken off and reached an altitude of about eleven hundred feet. I had finished an orange juice and a few handfuls of peanuts and was just dozing off when a thud jolted me awake. At first I thought we had hit something, but then I realized there had been an explosion. I could see a shower of sparks spewing from the left engine like a Roman candle on the Fourth of July.

The alarms were going off on the control panel, and red lights for all systems of the left engine were flashing—gages plunged to zero. Yet there was no sudden loss of altitude, and the right engine continued to function. The pilot immediately shut off fuel to the left engine to prevent a fire and external explosion. He was calm, working to maintain stability with one engine and, at the same time, radioing the tower for clearance to return to the strip.

I did not feel panic or extreme fear. My life did not "flash before me." I thought how blessed I'd been, how rich my life had been, and how much I would like to finish things I'd started. But I felt no impulse to beg for more of life, for I felt I'd already had more than my share.

It did occur to me we had just spent five hours taking pictures we might not need. And I thought about the puppy, about the note that lay that moment on the kitchen counter, telling the kids that finally we could pick him up when I got home. What a bittersweet note that would be if something like this marred the day and the memory! I hoped someone would see that Benjy got his puppy anyway.

There was what seemed like plenty of time . . . too much time . . . turning around, descending to a lower altitude, lining up with the runway, shooting the approach—all things we'd done dozens of times before. But this time I noticed every detail, was aware of every unfamiliar sound in the one remaining engine, experienced a special joy in feeling the landing gear go down and lock into place, felt the thud of rubber on pavement. Taxiing in was the hardest because, with only one engine, the plane kept trying to turn left. But Steve was a champ and took it all the way to the terminal safely.

We did some phoning. I called Bill, booked the 7:50 A.M. commuter to Indy, and found us rooms at the Sheraton. I crawled into bed at 1:18 P.M. and woke at 6:00 A.M. I did not lie awake thinking about it. I did thank God for water to wash my body, a bed to collapse into, and the sheer joy of being alive . . . and I slept.

Now we begin our descent into Indianapolis on this small Allegheny/US-Air commuter. If it's nice at home, I'll plant some flowers, feel the earth between my fingers, spend some time planning the tomorrows I may have . . . then the kids and I will go get our puppy.

June 6 — New York

One of the greatest bargains still available is the twenty-five-cent ferry fare from Manhattan to Staten Island, and this trip was what Amy and I chose to do with one of our precious evenings together in New York.

This journey, taken at sunset, rivals the experiences offered by the theater district of Broadway, the cultural offerings of Lincoln

Center or the newest creations of the fashion industry. For quadruple the price of this fare, one can purchase a giant ice cream cone before leaning against the turnstile that counts you as a "paid fare" and entering the wide boat called the *John F. Kennedy.*

The trip is a kaleidoscope of sights, a smorgasbord of smells and tastes, and an amusement park of sensations: people of every shade, size, and age, conversing excitedly in a symphony of dialects; the smell of sea and fuel mixed with the hot dogs and popcorn aroma rising from the concession stand in the center of the boat, the stifling humidity of a small space with too many bodies relieved by making one's way to the outer decks and the evening wind surprising the face and nostrils.

A black flutist stands in the fore part of the cabin with his instrument case open at his feet for donations. The sweet melody he plays softens the atmosphere and gently releases the tension of the work-pressured city dwellers. The musician plays with his eyes shut, isolating himself somewhere away with his music.

Soon the fore deck is crowded. An Oriental father lifts his pixie child up to peer through the coin-operated telescope, while the mother snaps pictures with her Minolta camera.

The whistle whines through the evening humidity and the ferry lunges forward, away from the dock. Bodies crowd the right-hand rail in anticipation of the Statue of Liberty. We can see that the scaffolding she has worn like a hairnet for the last year or two has been taken away and the torch is back in hand, held aloft like the giant lemon ice cream cone the Puerto Rican boy beside me holds just out of reach of his smaller sister.

Inside the boat, lazy city kids and bored businessmen sleep or read the evening paper. They are second and third generation Americans whose appreciation of this symbol has been dulled by too many years, too many crossings. But out here, families chatter enthusiastically in Spanish, Japanese, German, and Italian about the Lady. telling stories to their children of "coming here" or explaining how she came to guard the harbor.

I go several times to find Amy, who is talking ballet with her friend from Tennessee inside where the night air won't ruin their French braids. I try to tell her of the drama, its emotional roots centuries deep, that is being enacted out on the deck. But she mumbles something about it being "too crowded and windy," and I choose not to press her with explanations and sermons on "liberty."

I don't tell her that "crowded" is just what I want her to see and that "windy" isn't one of the hardships I want her to remember with her great-grandparents who came through this harbor from Italy, Germany, and Ireland. I just walk slowly back toward the crowded doorway and throw two quarters into the musician's flute case, then watch silently with the others as the crimson sun sets behind a symbol . . . and an age.

July 11 — home, at the creek

I am alone. Luscious solitude. The willows make a lacework canopy and drape around the gazebo where I hide, letting in the fickle breezes while keeping out intruders.

I wait silently and listen . . . to the sounds of July after the storm, to thoughts that too long have been shoved out to the periphery, and to my heart.

Activities and obligations have taken Bill and the children to safe and happy places today, leaving me this incredibly rare moment of worry-free solitude. I am experiencing not the "empty nest" syndrome—for our nest could never be empty, so crowded it is with memories, artifacts, and music left behind to fill each corner and ring through each corridor—but the "quiet nest" syndrome. This is not a *phenomenon* but a *place* one comes to, escorted by the finishing of much-loved and well-executed assignments of living.

That is it! I don't feel banished to loneliness but awarded by life to this wonderful solitude, and I revel in it today.

August 14 — Nantucket

We had such a great day yesterday at surfside; already I am sad about leaving this island. Each time we come here, the fabric of the memories takes on a different texture. By now the large pieces have been stitched into a growing comforter that warms and covers us all when days are cold and emotions are sore from being battered by the world.

This morning I am at the Blueberry Muffin waiting for Suzanne. Summer-tanned college students come in this place, some vacationing here before returning to the books, others working here for the summer.

There are women who come here alone. Perhaps some are vacationing with their families as I am and are simply early risers who treasure their solitude. But I suspect more are divorced or widowed and come here to be comforted by memories of happier times.

A few live here in the summer while their husbands commute, but the older, sea-worn, sun-freckled types are here alone, returning to the "summer place" from habit and the hope of finding here a place to belong. Nearly all have money, for it is very expensive to live here and maintain. (There is much effort spent on caring for and preserving everything, so there are few evident signs of struggle or deprivation.)

The kids, though dressed casually, are dressed in "careless chic" with long, baggy "Polo" sweats or purposely faded Laura Ashley skirts and carefully battered Gucci watches and bags. There is a look of "too much too soon" in their eyes and a longing to find anything that matters. Most are artificially cheerful, working hard at having fun, yet quite cynical about much beyond the now.

If Suzanne doesn't come soon, I will have to leave. The people waiting at the door are wanting my table; they watch me like I'm a candidate for a heart transplant donation. The early comers have given way to the "after eight o'clock" breakfast people, the impatient city dwellers who have long since forgotten how to wait, to submit, or prefer anyone else. They are brash, they are rich, and they're in a hurry.

August 16 — Nantucket

Today we leave. It was great to feel the surf pound against my body and lift me up with its power, to feel the cold current against my sore muscles (sore from long walks in the sand and bicycling.) Everyone has gotten along so well, a healthy mixture of ages and interests blending community with solitude, sometimes pairing off or choosing the intimacy of three or four.

It has been a fulfilling time with one exception—the part of me that needs to be fed on solitude still feels hungry. And sometimes I wish for time to walk in the foam at night with Bill or hold one another in some deserted cove where breezes from the sea blow gentle 'cross our skin.

But it's been good, and I will savor what I have: friendships, the joys of watching children grow and think and see things for themselves, the love of one good man who gives himself to making rich the moments that we have.

December 24 — home

Christmas Eve. Sitting by the Christmas tree with only the sparkling lights to see by . . . Amy and Suzanne asleep already by the tree, Benjy just getting home from the studio where he played acoustic guitar on a recording of "How Great Thou Art" for Jeff Silvey's grandma. Benjy was so excited. He wants to give his grandmas copies, too.

It's been fun watching these babies grow up, each year making little nests of pillows and blankets under the Christmas tree, reading "'Twas the Night Before Christmas" by the tree light and trying so hard to stay awake.

Each year I've gone to bed to listen for the silence of excited little voices, then the even measured breathing of children overtaken by sleep. Then I would get up and sneak to the

basement to stuff stockings and hang them bulging on
the fireplace, then fall exhausted into bed, cold and sleepy.

The next thing I'd know, there would be giggles and whispering
from the kitchen, then little voices urging us to get up.

Now the bodies sleeping around the tree fill up all the floor
space around the living room. Yet the magic of expectation and
the nostalgia of many beautiful memories crowd around to make
sleep hard to come by and storytelling a ritual. They sleep now,
these child-adults, these full-grown bodies I used to hold and rock
to sleep in my arms.

The rockers are still now, but the bodies are never still. They
dance and play guitars and move hurriedly across campuses. Still
I wait this Eve of Christ to hear the measured breathing so that I
can steal away to stuff stockings, then fall into bed.

The dogs sleep as near to us as they are allowed. The fire
crackles in the kitchen. The dim light from a hundred tiny lights
creates shadows of candles and poinsettias on the wall and on this
journal. I write . . . and wait. There is love here. I am so blessed
and I am thankful.

December 31 — home

Dear Suzanne:

From the moment I first held you in my arms still drenched in
birth until now as I watch you drive away to the appointments
you've made with life, mothering you has been my life's most
awesome, fearsome, and joyful adventure. I didn't know that
first day what mothering would mean, though I was eager to
begin.

You seemed so fragile then, so small and trusting, depending
on me for every life-sustaining need. I thought at first you'd
break: "Be sure to support the little head," they told me.

But I was soon to learn that you were tougher than you
looked—and could outsqueal, outsleep, and outendure me ten to

one. In fact, those first three months I wondered if I'd ever finish a meal or a night's sleep again as long as I lived.

The teaching began immediately. I had studied to be a teacher, but there was never a classroom student as hungry to learn as you. Before you could speak, your eyes asked the questions and your tiny hands reached to touch and learn, taste and see. It wasn't long, though, until your cooing turned inquisitive, with every babbled sentence ending with a question mark. Your first words were: "What's that? What's that?"

Soon your questing vocabulary grew, and you were begging, "Teach me something, Mommy. Teach me something." And I would stop to teach you: numbers, names of things, textures, shapes, sizes, foods, furniture, pets, trees, flowers, stars, and clouds. But soon you were teaching me—teaching me that when the lesson stopped, the learning kept on going.

You taught me to see the miracles I'd stumbled over every day. You taught me trust and delight and ecstasy. You held a mirror up before my attitudes and role-played all my reactions. You taught me what it meant to live what I verbalized, to believe what I preached, to internalize what I lectured.

You, who came to me all wet from birth, baptized the common things with natal freshness; with the shower of your laughter you washed away the barnacles of grownup cynicism and the dust of dull routine. You made things new. You gave me an excuse to be myself again, to skip down forest trails or sled the frozen hillsides clean with snow, to splash through springtime puddles, barefoot glad, and guess at where the shooting stars must go.

You gave me eyes to see the realness of people once again, to look beyond their faces' thin façades. You saw the child inside the aged, the longing and the passion long entrapped by gnarled joints and failing eyesight. You recognized profundity and wisdom in the giggly teenaged baby-sitter, beauty in the plain, and creativity in the timid. You showed me that the generation gap is the artificial invention of our culture and bigotry a sick perversion of nature's celebration of variety.

I have helped you learn to crawl, toddle, walk, run, swim, dance, ride bikes, and drive the car. I have encouraged you to stand tall, walk alone, run from evil, dance for joy, ride out the hard times, and drive yourself on when you felt tempted to give up. I have been there waiting when you crossed the road, climbed off the school bus, came in from dates, and returned home from college. In fact, now about all I can do for you is to be there, because gradually you have come to be your own person—not so much my child as my friend.

1987

There is always newness to be found in me,
and if I am learning something for the first time,
then I am Eve in Eden to my soul. . . .

January 23 — home

What can I say to this empty page that would, if not shake the foundations of history, then at least change the shape of this moment? How can I illuminate with the beacon of my words some miracle half-hidden by the mediocrity of this Friday in January or perhaps uncover some fossil of truth that has lain buried by the silt of outgrown cultures, excavate to the bedrock of the essential with my shovel of quest?

"There is nothing new under the sun," some wise Solomon has said, but there is always newness to be found in me, and if I am learning something for the first time, then I am Eve in Eden to my soul. I carry within me the dawn of every truth, and Genesis is not past but present every morn.

And the journey continues . . .